A CONSCIOUS PERSON'S GUIDE

TO RELATIONSHIPS

A Conscious Person's Guide to Relationships

Ken Keyes, Jr.

Second Edition

LIVING LOVE PUBLICATIONS

This book may be obtained through your local bookstore. Or you may order it from Ken Keyes College Bookroom, 790 Commercial Ave., Coos Bay, Or 97420 for $5.50 plus $1.25 for postage and packing.

First Edition		
First Printing		50,000
Second Printing		100,000
Second Edition		
First Printing		25,000
Second Printing		25,000
Third Printing		25,000
	Total	225,000

Library of Congress Cataloging-in-Publication Data
Keyes, Ken.
    A conscious person's guide to relationships.
    1. Love 2. Intimacy (Psychology) 3. Interpersonal relations. I. Title.
BF575.L8K46 1986   158'.2   86-27179
ISBN 0-915972-07-7 (pbk.)

LIVING LOVE PUBLICATIONS
700 Commercial Avenue
Coos Bay, Oregon 97420

This book is dedicated to the
heart-to-heart power of love
that can harmonize
our individual human differences—
and allow us to create
a great adventure of life
together.

CONTENTS

Part One
Seven Guidelines for Going Into
a Relationship

Part Two
Seven Guidelines for Creating
a Delightful Relationship

Part Three
Seven Guidelines for Altering Your Involvement

Part Four
Loving Unconditionally

Acknowledgments

There is no way for me to acknowledge every source of the wisdom that I have tried to package into this book. In one degree or another, perhaps everyone that has lived on earth has played a part in creating the experience of human life. All of us have helped to discover and demonstrate the lessons that our lives are offering us of what to do and what not to do to get the most from our lives.

Carole Thompson Lentz, Director of Cornucopia in St. Mary, Kentucky, has generously contributed excerpts from her sharings at Cornucopia workshops. The residents of Cornucopia have assisted in many ways. Their book, *The Methods Work . . . If You Do!* (which we use in workshops at Cornucopia and various cities throughout the nation) has been most helpful. The glossary in Appendix I has been largely taken from the *Methods* book. My heartfelt appreciation goes to Lenore Sheets, who transcribed and indefatigably typed the many revisions of the manuscript. Debra Bidwell generously helped with the typing. I also wish to express my appreciation to Ellen Wayne, Joe Newton, Joel Moskowitz, Kent Westbrook, Lenore Schuh, Lenore Sheets and Rick Wayne for their helpfulness, their insightful suggestions and their constant love during the period when I was writing and revising the manuscript.

Many thanks are due to Stuart Emery and his book, *Actualizations: You Don't Have to Rehearse to Be Yourself,* which I found inspiring. People who helped by giving me the benefit of their reactions to the manuscript include Bill Garvey, Bill Lentz, Char Cornucopia, Debbie Laughter, G. B. Cornucopia, Hedda Lark, Jai Michael Josefs, Marjorie Tully, Mark Allen, Shakti Gawain, Shirley Lewis, Tolly Burkan and Wade Laughter.

I also want to thank Britta Zetterberg for her contributions to the revised edition of this book.

The Twelve Pathways have been reprinted from my *Handbook to Higher Consciousness,* fifth edition, which was copyrighted in 1975 by Living Love Center.

Ken Keyes, Jr.
Coos Bay, Oregon

Introduction

Most of us are looking for a relation-SHIP that will carry us securely across the ocean of separateness to the beautiful shores of love, joy and happiness. Since divorce statistics show that about half of the people who begin the journey are abandoning ship, and the popular jokes about male-female relationships suggest that many others would like to, it may pay off handsomely to increase our skill in making this voyage.

This book contains seven guidelines for going into a relationship in a way that will give you the most growth and enjoyment. It also explains seven additional guidelines that can make your relationship richer and more delightful. It is primarily directed toward relationships that have the deeper involvement of living together—but the guidelines are universally applicable to relationships with children, brothers, sisters, parents, in-laws, friends, bosses, employees, etc.

I would like to say that if you read this book, you will live happily ever after. But this would be a lie, and lies are not helpful in getting the most from our lives. So-o-o-o, life being the way it is, in case the relation-ship doesn't work out, this book contains seven guidelines for altering your involvement in a relation-ship—another way of saying, "We aren't together anymore."

This book is based on my *Handbook to Higher Consciousness.* The *Handbook* describes the Living Love Way which shows you how to do something you never thought possible. It gives you precise methods for creating a fulfilling and happy life in a way that does not depend on other people changing their behavior! And it works! Thousands of people have taken Living Love workshops, and hundreds of thousands have read the *Handbook.*

I hope you find this book exciting, stimulating, and energizing. I want to quickly get into the twenty-one guidelines. But there is something we need to look at before we can go on.

I want to introduce the words "addiction" and "preference" so that we can use them as tools for communicating about life. We are all familiar with such statements as "He has a nicotine addiction." Now let's greatly expand our use of this word so that it becomes a useful tool in discovering things about ourselves. When we use the word "addiction," we will be referring to something we tell ourselves **we must have to be happy.** If we don't have it, we will feel emotionally upset.

In other words, **an addiction is an emotion-backed demand, model or expectation.** For example, if I get angry when you keep me waiting, I am in touch with an addiction. My feelings of anger, fear, frustration or any separating emotions are the tip-off as to whether or not I am addicted. I can tell whether I have an addiction by my gut-level feelings—not by looking at what people are saying or doing.

An addiction automatically creates our unhappiness when the world is not fitting our emotion-backed models of how things should be. Consciousness growth involves upleveling addictions to preferences—so that life situations do not trigger upsetting, separating responses. This gives us more insight, more choice and more rapport with people so that our lives work much better.

Addictions create your feelings of separation and unhappiness; preferences never do. When your addictions aren't satisfied, you automatically trigger irritation, resentment, fear, anger, worry, frustration, jealousy, boredom, etc. **You make yourself unhappy—but you create feelings inside you that the world is making you unhappy.** Addictions thus make you create lots of misleading illusions in your life. They keep your life in turmoil.

When you uplevel an addiction to a preference, it's a different story. When life satisfies your preference, you can create experiences of enjoyment, fulfillment, happiness and love. When life doesn't meet your preference, instead of creating unpleasant feelings such as fear, frustration or anger, you just feel relaxed and aware. You feel on a deep level, "I can accept it here and now because it's only a preference."

Thus a preference is a desire that does not make you upset or unhappy if it is not satisfied. The difference between an addiction and a preference has nothing to do with what's happening outside of you. The difference is in your **internal emotional**

experience. Upleveling an addiction to a preference doesn't necessarily require a change in your actions, opinions, models or thoughts. When you use preferential programming to create your experience of the here-and-now, you emotionally accept what is happening in your life because preferential programming does not make your ego push your emotional alarm buttons. With a preference, you might put a lot of energy into changing the outside world, but you are not addicted to the results of your actions.

Preferences enable you to enjoy yourself, other people and the life situation around you without being threatened when life throws changes your way. Everything that exists is in a process of flux and change. Some things change rapidly like the weather. Other things change slowly like the wrinkles on your face. To feel at home in this world, you must avoid being addicted to the status quo. Your mind must learn to hold on tightly—but let go lightly so you can flow with the tides of life.

When you work on your addictions and uplevel them to preferences, you do not have to be unhappy any longer. You do not have to change your opinions about life, you do not have to stop trying to change "what is" and you do not have to necessarily like "what is." **It's just that you no longer live with your finger stuck on the emotional panic button.**

Handling your addictions opens your heart to loving everyone unconditionally—including yourself. What you love is the person—just because they're there. For in their essence, they're just like you: they have a human heart and human feelings, and are really trying to make their life work.

Did you know that love is more important than anything else in your life? Security, delightful sensations, and success bring us certain satisfactions, but without the experience of love for yourself and others, your life will remain unfulfilling, basically lonely and you will miss the essence of it all. Your mind has so many ways to resist love—and to create the illusion of separateness. When you turn your perception and motivation so that you put love first, your life takes on a new dimension. Nothing else can be as continuously satisfying. Every person and everything is transformed as you increasingly create and maintain an inner experience of love and oneness. That's what this book is all about.

Now that we have briefly talked about turning down your addictions and turning up your love, we are ready to look at the seven guidelines for going into a relationship.

Part One

Seven Guidelines
for Going Into
a Relationship

1

Develop a Relationship With Yourself Before Getting Deeply Involved With Anyone Else.

If you addictively need a relationship, you're in trouble. In various ways, you are probably undermining your relationship. If you take two dominoes and lean them against each other, you have an unstable setup. If one of them moves, the other falls. If you create the experience that you are only half a person and you need someone to somehow help you fill in the missing half, your life won't work very well.

Your relationship may give you the illusion of working for a while. But when both of you eventually drop your phony fronts that hide your real feelings, you'll find that your partner cannot make you feel good and love yourself. Count yourself fortunate if your partner can do this for himself or herself!

In the past, you "bought into someone's stuff" when they told you that you were not beautiful, capable or lovable. (The glossary in Appendix I has definitions of special words or phrases.) All of this is nonsense, of course. You just handcuffed yourself with the models of people around you. You just laid on yourself a heavy bunch of "shoulds," "should nots" and "ought tos" that kept you telling yourself how inadequate you were. You're telling yourself that you would be lovable if you were "good." But the facts are that you are beautiful, capable and lovable the way you are. You will begin to let yourself experience this when you see through your addictive models of how you should be.

No dog would do to itself what you are doing to yourself. A little dachshund doesn't go around thinking it is inferior because it doesn't have the long legs of a greyhound. Greyhounds don't down themselves by saying, "I'm a failure. I'd have it made if I were short and cuddly and could sit on someone's lap like a dachshund." It takes a rational mind to do this hatchet job on oneself. No apple wishes that it were a banana, and no banana creates a feeling of inferiority because it's not like an apple. And the apples are not sitting around wishing they were big like watermelons. They're O.K. the way they are—and so are you. The only reason you don't feel O.K. is that you're telling yourself you ought to be different.

So don't be in too big a hurry to get involved with someone. Work on yourself first. You don't need another round of in and out that gives your ego and mind more illusory "evidence" of how inadequate and incapable you are. You also don't need a relationship to build "evidence" of how adequate or capable you are. You are absolutely beautiful the way you are—and the world has a place for you.

You may prefer to live in a relationship, but you'll make yourself miserable if you are addicted to it. A part of your inner growth will be to develop your self-confidence and self-acceptance. For many of us, this will take a lot of inner work. But what better way to invest your energy than to put it into yourself! And there's really no other way. For any outer game you get going will be undermined by the illusions and lies you are telling yourself about you.

Your relationship is like a mirror—it reflects you back to you. Whatever you demand or require, your partner will often develop an opposite energy. For example, if you play the part of "helpless," your partner may consciously or unconsciously push you into being more independent; if you demandingly play an independent role, your partner may consciously or unconsciously want you to become more dependent on him/her. The need for inner work that you have long neglected may pop up quickly in a relationship. Living together is a deeper level of involvement than you have usually permitted yourself to have.

Dating, friendships and work relationships often don't even get near the deeper levels of hidden "infections" in your mind that we call "addictive demands." The addictive demands that you have acquired during your lifetime will keep you from enjoying your relationship to the fullest. Chapter five explains how to recognize them so you can develop the skill of handling them.

Plan to do as much of your personality growth as you can before getting into a relationship. You can't do it all before. But you can get such a wonderful start in this direction that it will be much easier for you to hang on when your mind creates separateness in your relationship.

Instead of jumping into a deep-level involvement such as marriage, your life may therefore be more fun in the long run if you hold out for a while and work on yourself. There are many books and growth centers that may help you uncover your inner beauty. If you feel attracted to the way of working on yourself described in this book, you may wish to pursue it further in my *Handbook to Higher Consciousness*. The *Handbook* explains in greater detail many of the points in this book. It describes Six Methods for upleveling an addiction to a preference. (Appendix II tells where to get Living Love workshops and Appendix IV shows how to order the *Handbook*.)

So if you are creating the experience that you addictively need a relationship, you're going to put a burden on the relationship that could decrease the love feeling or blow it apart. And all of your self-rejection is one big illusion because you are whole and complete—just as you are. You may not be a banana—but you are a fine apple or pear. And being a fine apple or pear is enough. But you've got to believe this and feel this. If you don't feel you're enough, you'll project feelings of inadequacy, dependency and "Oh, poor me." Then your partner may buy into your illusion that you're not enough. So work on yourself until you know you can make it alone. Introduce yourself to the beautiful, capable and lovable you. Then let others discover you!

2

Go Into a Relationship to Cooperate With Each Other in the Great Adventure of Life.

If you wish to minimize pain and maximize satisfaction in a relationship, it is helpful to be clear on what you are seeking. Of course, anything that motivates you is O.K. I'm not saying that some motivations are right and some are wrong. What I'm saying is that the inspiration of "cooperating in the great adventure of life" may be helpful in increasing the joy and happiness in your relationship.

Many people don't seem to have a definite notion of what motivates them to go into a relationship. They seem to feel that the purpose of the relationship is the relationship itself. Yet most of us do have specific things in mind as we search around for a partner. See if you can identify with one or more of the following:

"I'd like to have a sexual partner."

"I feel more secure money-wise when I'm married to someone."

"It's really nice to have a companion so that I'm not lonely."

"It will make my parents feel better when I'm married."

"I want to have children."

"I can use my relationship for spiritual growth."

"I'm tired of dating around; it's time to settle down."

"I want someone I can show off to my friends."

"I need someone to earn money and take care of me if I'm sick."

"It helps me feel complete."

Let me again point out that I don't want to make any of the above ideas about going into a relationship either right or wrong. But I'd like to share with you what I tell myself in this area. Living with someone gives me the opportunity to cooperate in the great adventure of life. This tunes my mind in to an awareness of who likes to be with me and to cooperate in the things I enjoy doing. It also helps me look at whether I enjoy cooperating in the things she likes to do.

Of course, I don't expect anything to be one hundred percent—life isn't like that. I thank the universe if the person I'm living with likes to cooperate with me in three-fourths of the things I like to do in creating my adventure of living on planet Earth. As Goddard so beautifully put it, "Happiness is the art of making a bouquet of those flowers within reach."

Always remember that nothing will ever continuously fit our models of how things should be. Our minds can always envision a "should" or "ought to" pattern that no human being or relationship can possibly fulfill. Even when we wisely pick someone to cooperate with us in the great adventure of life, the day-to-day experience of living, working and playing together will always confront us with stuff we don't like. But we can breeze through this "win some—lose some" characteristic of human life by not creating a big crisis when we lose. We can just let things be the way they are, and not get ourselves upset by our models of perfection.

I also like the lift I get by looking at my relationship as a way of cooperating in the great adventure of life. It sets up an energy of fun and enjoyment. It suggests surfing through life—not plowing through it. When two people mutually wish to cooperate in the great adventure of life, all of the things we mentioned at the beginning of this chapter will have the best chance of automatically happening. All this—and heaven, too.

3

Falling in Love Is Not a Basis for Involvement.

"Falling in love is not a basis for involvement? That's crazy," you may say to yourself. I must admit that it does sound crazy—especially coming from the founder of the Living Love Way to happiness—but perhaps it's crazy wisdom.

The problem is that ninety-nine percent of us operate from a great deficiency of love. We often didn't experience enough love in our childhood, and our heart hungers for this precious feeling. We live continuously with this longing for love. We are on the lookout for people who seem to be able to accept and love us. We are like hungry tigers that haven't eaten for a month. And when we find a person who feels some love for us, it's a tremendous event. We feel love is so scarce that we have to do something about it. Cage it. Tie it up. Don't let it get away!

By using the Living Love Way in our lives, we can begin to create lives that are not deficient in love. We can learn to work on ourselves so that we clear away emotion-backed demands that other people be different from the way they are. As we reach behind the models in our minds, we can see the way in which each individual is beautiful, capable and lovable. By learning to accept people as they are, we can see the preciousness of each person. By working on our addictive models of how the world should be, we begin to radiate an ever-widening acceptance and love. The people around us begin to tune in to the way we are increasingly creating unconditional love for them. They like being with someone who is living love. It's like finding an oasis in the desert.

In my own experience, I found that as I learned to love unconditionally, I began to create and live in a world of love. I've now learned to operate my mind and heart so that I can stay in love with everybody—most of the time. And I work on my head quickly if my ego-mind hits me with an addictive model that throws me out of the love place. Since I am effectively working on my head, I cannot use love as a basis for involvement in a relationship because love becomes my general experience of almost everybody. I no longer live in a vacuum of love in which I am blown around whenever a breath of lovely fresh air comes in.

So if you are effectively working on yourself to love everyone unconditionally, you cannot use love as a basis for involvement. You'll be loving everybody—but you can't live with everybody you love.

We will often use the term "unconditional love" in this book on relationships. Let's make sure that we're clear on what this points to. Unconditional love is not the same as romantic love. Romantic love is a strong addictive attraction that is based on projecting onto another person our illusions of what we want in our lover. We don't love the individual with all of his or her "stuff"; we are only in love with an illusion created by our addictive desire systems.

Although romantic love is a great feeling, building a relationship on it is like building a house on quicksand—the foundation is not stable. Unconditional love gives a stable foundation to a relationship. And it means just what it says. No conditions—no strings attached to my love. No matter what you say or do, I will continue loving you. I may not like what you do, but my love is unconditional and will not be affected—not even if our involvement changes.

If we don't use love as a basis for involvement, what do we use? There are about four billion people on earth. How do we choose with whom to be involved? It's very simple. We choose to be involved with someone because we enjoy playing the same life games together. I'm not using "game" in the Eric Berne (*Games People Play*) sense of a dishonest ploy to mislead someone. I'm using the word "game" in its basic meaning as in "a game of checkers." From this point of view, we create the experience of life as a fun game to be played rather than a heavy load of problems to be solved.

When we approach life as a set of games to be played, we add juice to everything we do. A game is anything that has do's and don'ts reflecting our skill— and a way to tell when we reach the goal. Thus going to the movies can be experienced as a game. Making money is a game. Having children is a game. Growing in consciousness is a game. Getting married is a game; being married is an even more challenging game. Buying a new car is a game. Sex is a game. Getting sick is a game. Getting well is a game. And even dying is a game of life.

If a loving, conscious person were to use only love as a basis for choosing a partner, it would be like using the existence of a steering wheel for deciding what car to buy. Since all cars have steering wheels, we need other criteria for deciding. When you're doing a good job of handling your addictions and loving unconditionally, your life will be so filled with love! Then you can choose a partner because you like to play the same life games together—to celebrate life together. Thus love is no longer a guideline, for you are learning to love everyone unconditionally— including yourself.

4

Can You Share Life's Games in a Way That Will Contribute to Your Mutual Well-being?

In the course of a week, two people living together may make many contributions to each other's mutual well-being. These can take the form of energy put into helping one another by cooking, serving or dishwashing, housecleaning, yardwork, maintaining the car, assisting when sickness occurs, working to produce a flow of green energy, helping the children, playing host for friends, doing thoughtful things, suggesting a good book, movie or a concert and cooperating in sexual enjoyment.

In general, you contribute to your mutual well-being when you enjoy the "enoughness" that you do have in your life, and thus open your heart to happiness by not creating emotion-backed demands for what you don't have. Specifically, a deeper level of contributing to each other's well-being will include handling your own addictive emotion-backed demands, and creating emotional space for your partner to run off anger, fear, jealousy, irritation, resentment, depression and other separating emotional states (even when directed toward you). It can also include helping your partner do what s/he wants to do instead of what you think s/he ought to do, compassionately understanding tension areas with relatives or friends and non-aggressively sharing your innermost feelings—deeper and deeper. One of the greatest contributions is working on your addictions in order to love everyone unconditionally—including yourself.

It's realistic to recognize that whether we are single or double, it takes a lot of "doing" to operate a human life. And life's activities may be more fun when they are shared. But this joy of living together can only reach its highest fruition when our egos have insight into the physical, mental, emotional and spiritual richness that our relationship offers us. We usually look at what we don't have and ignore the "enoughness" of what we do have. We often blame our partner, and this always means we're running one of our addictions. We often focus on the additional things our partner "should" or "could" offer us in the relationship. Our logical intellect may addictively insist on a "fair" or a "50-50" approach. This just causes arguments in which we make ourselves "right"—but we lose intimacy and happiness.

Your ego may create the illusion that if you constantly point out the deficiencies of your partner, s/he will be motivated to give you more. You may have noticed that this isn't effective. You may try to bribe, coerce or shame him or her into giving you more than s/he is giving at the moment. This really won't work well, either. But if you're doing these things in your relationship, don't put yourself down. These "right-wrong" games of the ego-mind are only a stage of growth. Be gentle and compassionate with yourself.

To emotionally demand things of your partner is human; to let go of separating demands is divine. As you tune more deeply in to your spiritual wisdom which has often been lying unused in your heart, you will begin to realize that your partner can only be where s/he is at each moment. And if real change (instead of coerced, surface, phony change) is to take place, it is only through love that s/he will create more perceptiveness of your needs and desires, and more willingness to do what you want.

The best way to help your partner experience greater love is **for you to create in yourself an experience of greater love for him or her**—and I mean do it first. And I mean do it continuously. And I mean to keep doing it whether or not you get the "results" you are looking for. To really get "results," you must strip your love of all its conditionality. For love does not work when you expect to get something. You love a person because he or she is there—not because s/he needs, merits or deserves your love. When you love someone, you are tuned in to your beloved's relationship to his or her own life—and not narrowly concerned with his or her relationship to your life.

As you learn to radiate your love simply because it is the best way to be kind to yourself, this pure love will automatically produce the most that is obtainable in a relationship between two people. So you tell your ego-mind to relax and make it O.K. not to get everything you want. Because that's the way life is—you win some and you lose some.

So when you are considering going into a relationship, **look deeply into your heart to discover your level of commitment to the other person's well-being.** What are you willing to "be with" from day to day? There are some "gifts" you cannot afford to give. Be totally realistic—it's kindest in the long run. From time to time, your partner's well-being may need things on which you do not want to spend money, time or energy. If it really affects your partner's well-being, will your ego activate the paranoia of the separate-self, or do you want to work on yourself to flow your love and cooperative energy through your unified-self? What are your limits? And make it O.K. to have limits. Everyone has them—but they expand further and further as you grow in consciousness.

Time, space and energy are a gift from the

universe. But your separate-self ego may make you feel that it is "your time," "your space" and "your energy." The fulfillment of your life requires you to learn to give of these things freely. However, your ego often will not permit you to give these gifts without developing a feeling of resentment or a bookkeeping approach—"I've done this for you so you now owe me something."

Your selflessness will vary from person to person—and from time to time. And while it is beautiful to give, you can create the feeling of separateness if your ego keeps pointing out what you have given. The consistent winners in the love game learn to love and serve others without the self-consciousness that they—as separate individuals—are doing it.

So, in choosing someone to live with, it may be wise to ask if you feel that the unfolding of your life is in harmony with sharing life's games in a way that will contribute to the well-being of your partner as s/he sees his or her well-being. This means looking deeply into your heart and mind to see to what extent you can appreciate your relationship as an opportunity to love and serve your beloved. And this means giving him or her what s/he wants—not what you think s/he should want. There's a lot of difference!

5

Don't Expect the Relationship to Make You Happy.

The opportunity to live with another human being is one of life's greatest gifts. You damage and bruise this gift by your demands and expectations that the relationship make you happy. Sorry, but no one's going to rescue you. The number and strength of your addictions is far more important in creating your personal experience of happiness or unhappiness than who you're with!

The things that come up in a relationship tell you something about yourself. If you have few addictions, your relationship will give you the opportunity to create more happiness in your life. If you have lots of addictions, your relationship will give you the opportunity to get more in touch with your addictive hang-ups—which can temporarily create more unhappiness in your life. But since you always have the option of using these experiences for your growth, the friction in your relationship can help you make the rest of your life more enjoyable. All you need is your determination to skillfully use every life situation for your growth. Everyone, and everything, becomes your teacher.

You can create the experience of disillusionment and cynicism if you burden your relationship with the expectation of eliminating what you don't like about your life. If, for example, your addictions create a heavy experience of loneliness, or you create miserable feelings without sex, there is nothing your partner can do that will fully and continuously satisfy these emotion-backed demands in your life. The only thing that you can dependably expect from your relationship is the opportunity to use your life situations to uplevel your addictions to preferences, and to learn to emotionally accept what is here and now in your life. Then you will find that you always have "enough" in your life.

Emotionally accepting does not mean that you don't try to change something. It just means that you don't waste your energy in anger, irritation, resentment, fear and frustration. You accept without resistance what you can't change. And you intelligently focus your energy into making whatever changes are possible without setting up new problems in your life. You don't have to make yourself angry to work on changing what is wisely changeable. You can trust yourself to intelligently work on your preferences.

To understand why your relationship will not make you happy, we need to delve profoundly into the immediate, practical cause of unhappiness in an adult human life. So please hold on while we go into some basic principles of happiness in the remainder of this chapter. Your thorough understanding of these life-giving principles is needed to apply the relationship guidelines so you can fully benefit from them in your daily life. So let's look carefully at how you are controlled and dominated by your addictions—and how great it is to be free when you uplevel them to preferences.

As you grow in consciousness, you increasingly take responsibility for creating your moment-to-moment experience of life. **You stop accusing other people of doing it to you.** You see that outside events are what they are. Information on these events feeds in through your eyes and ears and other senses to the inner recesses of your brain. If you have addictive programming, it will trigger the emotional experiences that create separateness and unhappiness in your life.

If your relationship can't be relied upon to make you happy, then how does one go about creating a happy life? Let's explore the real causes of unhappiness in your life. **If you look closely at your life, you will see that your addictive, emotion-backed demands are the immediate, practical cause of unhappiness.** The following diagram shows how this works:

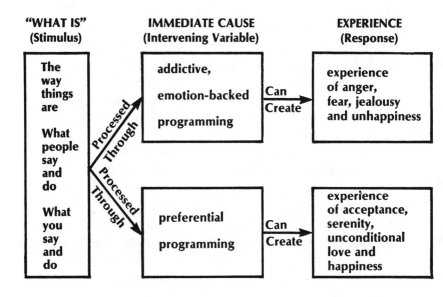

"WHAT IS" (Stimulus)	IMMEDIATE CAUSE (Intervening Variable)	EXPERIENCE (Response)
The way things are What people say and do What you say and do	addictive, emotion-backed programming Can Create	experience of anger, fear, jealousy and unhappiness
	preferential programming Can Create	experience of acceptance, serenity, unconditional love and happiness

If you understand the above diagram and verify it by carefully observing how your mind works, you can free yourself from the illusion that the outside world makes you afraid, frustrated, angry, irritated, jealous or unhappy.

This diagram shows how our internal emotional experience is created by our addictive or preferential programming. You'll recall that our addictions are emotion-backed demands that automatically make us trigger anger, irritation, fear, resentment, boredom, grief, etc. when life is not meeting the addictive models or belief systems in our heads. For example, if I'm addicted to your not criticizing me, and you say something critical, I automatically become angry. **The addiction is the cause of my anger; the anger is the effect of the addiction.** If I'm addicted to holding onto my money, I will automatically create the experience of self-rejection or irritation if I lose $10 from my pocket. If I am addicted to your always showing up promptly, I will, like a good addictive robot, make myself create the experience of hurt or disappointment if you are late.

Addictions are not good or bad—or right or wrong. They aren't like sin. It's O.K. to have an addiction. Don't be addicted to being without addictions. Just notice that addictions make you emotionally or intellectually reject yourself and others. They make you miss the fun of creating a happier life; they keep you from loving yourself and others. Addictions are not necessary since **we can prefer all of these things** instead of being addicted to them. And from a preferential space, we can put a lot of energy into making changes in our lives—and the world around us. We can trust ourselves; it's not necessary to drive ourselves with addictions to keep our lives together.

There is no way to consistently feel good with

23

addictions. When I don't get my addiction satisfied, I make myself unhappy. When I do get my addiction satisfied, I experience temporary pleasure but I become addicted to holding on to whatever is satisfying it. So I just add to the load of addictions I am carrying around. As the Third Patriarch of Zen put it, "To set up what you like against what you dislike is the disease of the mind."

Addictions make us reject "what is" in our lives and automatically trigger separating emotions. When we produce alienating emotions continuously, we make ourselves unhappy. Our addictive programming creates our illusory, distorted experience of situations by intermixing a narrow view of "what is" with our hopes, fears, memories of the past, concerns for the future; our emotional reactions of anger, fear, jealousy, hate, irritation and resentment; plus all the right-wrong rationalizing that our minds are so good at spinning out. Reality loses; mind-stuff wins.

Addictions are thus the enemy of happiness. When I look closely at each addictive demand that often seems so special, I usually discover that the general pattern of this addictive programming has caused me separateness and unhappiness for most of my lifetime. These addictions have not only harmed me in the past, they can also threaten my future if not handled.

Let's suppose I'm addictively demanding that people notice me and talk to me—and include me in what they're doing. These addictions can keep me vulnerable to running tapes of anxiety, fear, resentment, anger, irritation and other separating emotions. They can affect my body and create tension, uneasiness, sleeplessness and sometimes pain and illness. My addictive programming will stimulate my mind to run judgmental, critical and blaming tapes. My emotion-backed demands will be dominating my consciousness, and smother my love for myself and other people.

I could be enjoying my life if "getting attention and being invited" were preferences. (And I'd probably get more attention and invitations, too!) But whatever life gives me, preferences let me accept and love myself and others—even while I work to change some things.

Let's take an awesome look at the life-killing things that addictions do to us. By creating distorted perceptions, addictions affect our insight into what is happening in our lives. They make us unable to appreciate the beauty that is here and now, and they keep us trapped in illusory versions of "what is." When we uplevel these addictions to preferences, we can let ourselves enjoy our here-and-now. Addictions waste our energy in bodily tensions and emotional drains. Preferences enable us to release our energy to enjoy life and to creatively change what can be changed. When we work from preferential programming, we are able to focus our energy more effectively.

When we are stuck in addictive programming, we keep perpetuating certain patterns or problems in our lives that influence people to respond to us in certain set ways. Addictions also make us inflexible, block our creativity and make us worried and fearful. They create the illusory experience that life is a constant conflict. As addictions are upleveled into preferences, we tune in to a level of spontaneity, creativity and openness that lets us clearly look at "what is" in life and deal with it insightfully. Preferences let us see the melodrama of our life from a larger perspective—accepting what we can't change, and playing the game of changing what we can.

Addictions limit our alternatives and choices. They keep us trapped in "tunnel vision," in which we tend to respond automatically and have few options. Preferences enable us to see many beautiful choices in life, and to be open to a wide variety of possibilities. Addictions limit our ability to make changes in our lives. And even when we do make a change, addictions often create the experience that we still don't have "enough." Addictions make us continually escalate our demands.

We are unable to enjoy what we have because we are addictively protecting it for fear of losing it. Preferences enable us to enjoy what is now in our lives. They let us stay tuned to the ebb and flow of life so that we can love life the way it is—instead of continually struggling to make things fit the addictive models in our heads.

Our egos hold on to our addictive programming because we are willing to settle for certain payoffs— even though the overall effect of the addiction is that of creating separateness and unhappiness in our lives.

Some of the payoffs that keep us stuck in our addictive programmings are:

"I get to be right and make the other person wrong."

"I get to feel superior."

"I'll prove it's unfair or untrue."

"It feels safe and familiar to hold on to old programming, and scary to let it go."

"I get sympathy from other people who have the same addiction that I do."

"I feel really alive when I get angry."

"If I get angry enough, they may do what I want."

"They'll make it up to me because they'll see how upset I am, and they'll feel bad or guilty."

"I get to be unhappy and perhaps some people will feel sorry for me."

When we really look at the lost happiness, lost joy, lost closeness and lost love, we see that we are paying heavily for our addictions. We begin to see that these payoffs are a very poor substitute for the tuned-in aliveness and love we can create as we increasingly use preferential programming in responding to the here-and-now in our lives.

As you increase your understanding and skill with this expanded use of the word "addiction," you'll find it unfolding in a richer and richer way. It will help you consciously learn to be the creative cause of your experience of life (rather than a robot who is an effect of the surrounding world). You'll find that **the key to living a happy life lies in turning down your addictions and turning up your love.**

The way to intelligently operate your mind so that it does not keep jabbing you with anger, fear, frustration and unhappiness is to keep your addictive expectations well in hand. When you let go of the expectation that your relationship will make you happy or make disappear everything you don't like about your life, you can begin to appreciate the relationship for the richness that it does give you. The greatest richness is that you can absolutely count on your relationship to give you lots of opportunities for consciousness growth. Whether you use them or not is up to you.

In this chapter we have delved deeply into the nature of addictions. We have found that our addictions are the immediate, practical causes of our separateness and unhappiness. And we have seen that preferential programming is the answer to creating fun, enjoyment and love. We thus discover that it is unrealistic to expect our relationship to make us happy. No person or thing can make us happy. **It's up to us to make ourselves happy.** All our relationships can do is to furnish a cast of characters for our melodrama. It's up to us whether we run a preferential comedy or an addictive tragedy.

6

Can You Use the Relationship for Your Consciousness Growth—But Work O N L Y on Your Own Head?

Daily living with your husband or wife or children may be regarded as a testing ground. All of your addictive areas, such as your unresolved fears, the special privileges you want to hold onto and your inflexibilities in terms of money, pride and prestige, will sooner or later offer you a chance for growth. All of your "special stuff" that makes you vulnerable to creating the experience of separateness and alienation will be there to check you out sooner or later.

Your life experiences will give you the teachings you need to uplevel your addictions into preferences. Whatever security addictions you have that make you create the experience of fear, worry and anxiety will be there to be worked on. Retreating from situations and ignoring your addictive demands will not suffice in the give-and-take of living with someone. Or you may try the power approach and attempt to handle situations by bulldozing in like a Caterpillar tractor. But such a heavy-handed approach to life problems creates too much resistance and separateness.

The only thing that makes sense when living with your partner and your children is to work back and forth with the situations in your life. Your ego and mind often make situations appear solid and unworkable. "He never helps me." "She wastes too much money." But people are not set in concrete. They can change. However, the people in your life usually do not change immediately when you want them to. You need patience and a willingness to work with life as it is. It's O.K. to try to change things. But above all, continually use every situation for your own growth— while carefully watching your addiction that things should change faster than they are changing.

Perhaps your ego-mind had hoped to avoid coming to grips with your separate self, which is primarily concerned with the protection of your security, sensation and power addictions. But you may be getting tired of carrying your neuroses. So you begin to welcome the opportunity (even if painful) that your minute-to-minute experience offers you to become aware of the addictions you must reprogram to be liberated from your robot-like emotional patterns.

However, it may take a while before you are really ready to use this opportunity for the inner growth that living together offers. The ego may first try a diversionary strategy that does not require it to surrender any territory. You discover that it is easier to make a big deal out of your partner's addictions than to work on your own. Your ego often chooses to forget that consciousness growth is an individual matter. Although it's nice when it happens, you don't need a partner that works on his or her growth. You can work on your own growth and clean up the emotion-backed demands that make you feel so separate from yourself and others **without having a partner who is similarly engaged.**

Consciousness growth is not like checkers where two people have to know the rules and agree to play together. The Six Methods for consciousness growth described in the *Handbook to Higher Consciousness* offer you a way to work on yourself, and to use the parade of situations in your life for your own growth regardless of whether your partner does or not.

What I'm saying is that you can delay your growth for many years (or even a lifetime) if you insist on criticizing, analyzing and pointing out the emotion-backed demands of your partner when s/he is not asking you to do so. Such an aggressive attitude toward the addictions of your beloved permits you to ignore your own stuff. Your ego finds that the best way to defend itself is to attack. So, for your own growth, work only on your head and let your partner take responsibility for his or her growth—or lack of it. And remember, you can actually grow faster if your partner has addictions! Lucky you!

Thus, when you choose a partner, you take on the inner work of making the other person's hang-ups O.K. Suppose you are considering living with someone who is addicted to eating peanut brittle candy—and even munching on it in bed. Let's assume that you are minimizing the intake of white sugar in your diet, and you're avoiding those bulging fat banks that are such bad news in the insurance longevity statistics. Since you are obviously "right" on both of these dietary matters (to say nothing of the crumbs in bed), you may be tempted to "straighten out" your partner. But remember, while peanut brittle may bring on stomach upset, it does not cause anger; it's your addiction that is the immediate, practical cause of your anger.

Your ego may tell you that a bit of anger, irritation or resentment is well deserved—if not helpful to your friend. But such aggression may not be helpful to your own growth. You may, of course, wish to point out these things in a non-judgmental and loving way. But if your friend doesn't choose to work on the addiction for peanut brittle, it's up to you to take on the inner work of handling your own addiction that s/he change. The game is to see the situation as an opportunity that life is giving you to work on yourself to get free of the right-wrong judgmentalness that can be so separating and destructive of love.

In such situations, it is helpful to remember that your growth does not require you to rescue your friend from his or her peanut brittle addictions. The real growth game of life is to learn to love everyone unconditionally—and especially yourself. The peanut brittle is simply the grist for the mill of your consciousness growth.

When you work on your own addiction that your friend not eat so much peanut brittle, you'll find that you didn't have any real problem to begin with. If you can turn down your addiction and turn up your love enough, s/he may respond to your love by not eating peanut brittle in bed. But if it doesn't happen this way, you can feel good about having done what you could do from a loving space to change the situation. And either way you gain—for you have succeeded in your inner work in upleveling an addiction to a preference.

But your separate-self may not want to see it this way. You have to constantly confront it with the question, "Is it more important to create my inner experience of unconditional love for my beloved, or to try to addictively force him or her to quit eating peanut brittle?" Is anything really worth creating so much hurt, anger and separation between you and the person you love? Do you really think your partner wants to live with someone who is constantly pressuring? Is the pain and suffering you trigger in yourself and your loved one worth the change or concession that you might be able to force upon your partner? How long do the emotional wounds you create in yourself take to heal at your present level of skill in upleveling addictions to preferences? Is the thing you're wanting really worth running the risk of an addictive snarl that may be beyond your present ability to handle—a snarl which could make you alienate yourself from your beloved? (An addictive snarl is a set of strong, multiple addictions that enable your ego to blame the outside world and thus cop out on taking responsibility for your experience. A "snarl" distorts your perception of your life situation by a "right-wrong" attitude that makes you addictively cling, addictively reject or just ignore. We discuss what to do about snarls in Chapter 12.)

Life is much more enjoyable when your ego and mind learn to work on your addictions that are triggered by your partner's addictions. So when looking around for a partner for a relationship, find someone with whom you are willing to take on the inner work of making his or her addictions O.K. But be realistic. There are a lot of people that have addictions I am not willing to live with. I would not go into a relationship with a partner who gets drunk every day. I'm not willing to choose to work on my addictions that would be triggered. I try to at least set up my relationship for fun—and then I will work on what life gives me—which will be plenty!

7

"I Love You" Really Means "When I'm With You, I'm in Touch With the Beautiful, Capable and Lovable Parts of Me."

When going into a relationship, it is helpful to have a clear understanding of what the words "I love you" really mean. Of course, if you are a saint who has completed the inner work of upleveling addictions to preferences, the words "I love you" are more likely to be an expression of the oneness that is being experienced with everything everywhere. Since this book was not written for saints, let's look at what the rest of us mean by "I love you."

What is really happening inside my nervous system when I say, "I love you"? What's happening is that when I am with you, things you say and do **help me experience parts of me that I regard as beautiful, capable and lovable.** In other words, **what I am loving is my own experience of me.** You're mirroring me and are letting me see the beautiful, capable and lovable parts of me.

Now let's turn this around. If I create the experience of hating you instead of loving you, it means that the things you are doing and saying are more or less continuously putting me in touch with thoughts and actions that I would addictively reject in me if I were to say or do them. For example, if after much effort I finally manage to quit smoking, the sight of your smoking may touch off heavy addictive programming that makes me dislike you for smoking because I now reject this type of behavior in myself—or perhaps because being with smokers makes it difficult for me to resist my addiction. Perhaps a while back when I was smoking, I may have loved you for your smoking because it then reminded me of behavior I was still accepting in myself.

Thus we see that other people simply act as a mirror for what we are accepting or rejecting in ourselves. Unfortunately the illusion that we create through the operation of our minds is that **we credit the mirror (the other person) for what we see reflected there. The big game of the ego-mind is to keep us trapped in the illusion that its feelings and judgments refer to external realities.** We thus see that we create the experience of love or hate based on what we accept or reject in ourselves (or would accept or reject in ourselves if we were doing these things).

Since this is a rather sloppy and self-centered procedure for determining the quality and quantity of our love, we increasingly see how important it is to learn to accept and love ourselves—and I mean unconditionally. When we burden our perception of ourselves with all these shoulds and shouldn'ts, rights and wrongs, and goods and bads, we really destroy our ability to perceive other people clearly—and to create the experience of love when we are with them.

We thus see that when we reject someone, we are really rejecting something in ourselves—and we are thus blaming an innocent person. As we become more skillful in creating our experience, we increasingly learn to create the continuous experience of ourselves and others as beautiful, capable and lovable. As we become more aware of the inner workings of our minds, we increasingly understand how "I love you" basically means, "When I'm with you, I get in touch with those parts of me that I experience as beautiful, capable and lovable."

There are over four billion people on this earth. So how do we choose whom to be involved with? Obviously, selection is needed. It makes sense to get to know your own addictive demand patterns and those of the person you're thinking of being with. In a relationship, you'll have to live with each others' addictive demands. You have to ask yourself if you can be with his/her demands for the rest of your life.

I strongly recommend that you don't go into a relationship with a secret program in your head that you're going to change the other person so that you can live happily with him/her. I've tried it and it doesn't work! There's nothing wrong with asking a person to change. But if you must have someone change in order for you to be happy, you're just setting up trouble in your life.

It's O.K. to be selective when deciding on a partner. Some people's addictive demands will be easier for you to live with than others. But above all, develop your body, mind and loving spirit so you don't blow apart when strong emotions are triggered.

Don't fall into the trap that there is only one special person that you are able to love. Instead, try to develop the expectation that the world is full of people that you can love and that can love you—even in the deeper levels of relationships. Since "I love you" really means "when I'm with you, I'm in touch with the beautiful, capable and lovable parts of me," you will greatly increase the number of people with whom you can establish a deep love relationship **by more deeply accepting and loving yourself!**

Since your partner is a projection in your mind of what you want and don't want in your life, the simplest way to change your experience of your partner is to work on what you're judgmentally rejecting about yourself. This neat strategy involving your own inner development can make you the master of your experience—instead of being an effect of the person you choose to be in a relationship with. This helps you to stay out of the dead end you get yourself into when you create the illusion that you've got to find the one person that is your soul mate—and on whom your happiness depends.

Now that we've looked at seven guidelines for going into a relationship, we're ready for the next step—seven guidelines for creating a delightful relationship.

Part Two

Seven Guidelines
for Creating a
Delightful Relationship

8

Involvement, Yes; Addiction, No.

To get the most from your relationship, you'll find it helpful to distinguish between **involvement** with a person and **addiction** to being with the person. Let's define these two key terms. Involvement means "I share my life with you." Addiction means "I create the experience that I am lost without you. I need you to be happy."

Involvement means spending a lot of time together. Addiction means creating emotion-backed demands in my head that dictate what my partner should say and do—it means "ownership." Involvement means that I choose to share a large part of my life with my beloved and build a mutual reality together. Addiction means that I feel insecure without someone—I want him or her to save me. My involvement gives me the opportunity to experience all of the beautiful, loving things that a relationship can bring into my life. It also lets us shoulder together the responsibilities and problems of life and develop a mutual trust. Addiction opens a can of worms that makes me tarnish the beauty of my relationship. It makes me impose a lot of emotion-backed models of how my partner should be for me to let myself be happy.

Since involvement offers us the deeper enjoyments of a relationship, and addiction leads to misery in a relationship, let's look more closely at how involvement and addiction interact. It's possible to have a relationship in which there is:

1. Maximum involvement and maximum addiction.
2. Minimum involvement and maximum addiction.
3. Minimum involvement and minimum addiction.
4. Maximum involvement and minimum addiction.

Since these four possibilities create varying degrees of heaven or hell in a relationship, let's find out how you can set up your relationship so that it can be as heavenly as possible. But first, remember that I am talking about your own involvement and your own addictions. It does not refer to what your partner says or does. Instead it puts the spotlight on how you are operating your head. And this is good news. Any approach to getting the most out of life that depends on manipulating or changing another person is ultimately doomed to fail. But when you know how **to succeed within yourself,** you have all the aces in your hand. Actually it's only **your mental habits that stand between you and your continuous enjoyment of the**

melodrama of your life.

Let's look at setup number one—**maximum involvement with maximum addiction.** In this state you have deeply involved your life with the life of another person. You are living with your partner, and are usually with him or her many hours each day. You are addicted to being with this person. You have "territorial" feelings toward your beloved; you have many emotion-backed demands of how this person should act to fit your models. We often call this situation "romantic love." Once the romance is killed by addictions, what's left is just "possessive love."

Romantic or possessive love is unstable and tends to be emotionally explosive. Frequently heard are such statements as "If you really loved me you would . . . ." (fill in your addictive demand). This romantic-possessive aspect of the maximum involvement and maximum addiction phase keeps you yo-yoing up and down. You're very happy when things are fitting your addictions; you're very unhappy when they aren't. And in this phase, love is highly conditional. I love you when you meet my addictive models, and I'm rejecting you when you don't. Romantic or possessive love can create beautiful feelings at times. But it is a bumpy road—often with a washout at the end.

Now let's look at what happens when you have **minimum involvement and maximum addiction.** This is when the tears get to flow in your soap opera. It's usually called "broken heart." Minimum involvement means that you do not spend much time (or any time) with the other person, but you're still creating the experience that your happiness depends on being with him or her. Minimum involvement and maximum addiction sets you up for triggering disillusionment, cynicism, anger, resentment and the whole Pandora's box of separating emotions. Although you're not involved in living together, your mind can still produce an intense experience of jealousy.

A third type of situation occurs when there is **minimum involvement and minimum addiction.** It's often called "good friends." Since minimum involvement means that you're not spending much time together, you're not tuning in to the richer veins of human experience that more involvement offers. However, you're not creating a lot of stuff either, since your mind is not playing out heavy addictions about how the relationship should be. With minimum involvement and minimum addiction, your relationship is generally a light and pleasant one.

It's the fourth state that gives you all of the goodies of a deep relationship and none of the unhappiness. This is characterized by **maximum involvement and minimum addiction.** In this state, you consciously enjoy the relationship and realistically play the relationship game. By living together and having the opportunity to more deeply participate in each other's thoughts and feelings, you have the greatest opportunity to create all of the beautiful sharings that the relationship can bring you. And yet by minimizing your addiction, you do not keep the here-and-now muddied up with emotion-backed demands that your partner say and do things differently.

In this ideal state, your love is less and less conditional. You can communicate with your partner and tell him or her what you prefer in the relationship. But you quickly work on yourself to handle any addictions you are creating that can chip away at your feelings of love. You get to cooperate in the great adventure of life together and to contribute to each other's well-being.

Here's a chart that can be helpful in sorting out how involvement and addiction interact to determine the quality and quantity of your relationship.

INVOLVEMENT	ADDICTION	WHAT'S HAPPENING
Maximum	Maximum	**Romantic or Possessive Love**
Minimum	Maximum	**Broken Heart**
Minimum	Minimum	**Friends**
Maximum	Minimum	**All The Goodies. No Unhappiness.**

The importance of working on your addictions is spotlighted by what I'm going to call the "law" governing relationships: **IF YOU DON'T HANDLE YOUR ADDICTIONS, YOU'LL AUTOMATICALLY DECREASE YOUR INVOLVEMENT.** From this it follows that to maintain a high level of involvement or to increase your involvement, you must handle your addictions. Now you've got the key to living "happily ever after"—or at least knowing what the problem is!

9

Work to Communicate Deeper and Deeper Levels of Both Inner and Outer Honesty.

Let's distinguish between inner and outer honesty. Outer honesty simply means that we are no longer lying to our partner. A lie is a deliberate attempt to deceive. Outer honesty means not saying things we know are untrue. Most of us have discovered that lying can create a lot of problems. Sooner or later we will be caught in a lie—it's embarrassing and trust is undermined.

There is no way that you can get the most from your relationship if trust is lacking. And when you tell a lie, you must always remember exactly what lie you told and who you told it to—or you'll trip up later. The desire to lie is always created by your addiction and thus furnishes a clue to the next step in your inner work. To create the most loving and joyful experience in living with your beloved, you may wish to stop doing things you are not willing to share. **It's O.K. to think anything—but share it.** The world frowns on lying and deceiving, and most of us who are into consciousness growth have our outer honesty game in a pretty good shape.

Your greatest challenge as a human being lies in the development of **a deeper and deeper level of inner honesty.** Inner honesty in a living-with relationship means totally opening yourself by sharing your deepest feelings with your partner. If you're not deeply honest and open, what people are relating to is your "act"—it's not you. Inner honesty means trusting that you are naturally lovable when you are being yourself. If you are unable to share your inner thoughts, it means that you view yourself as separate from your beloved. You don't trust and love yourself enough to be honest about your feelings. Yet your life is trying to tell you over and over again that separateness and hiding are not the way to get the most turned-on enjoyment from your relationship.

It takes a lot of inner work on yourself to develop a high level of inner honesty in your relationship. Your ego may try to barter and say, "I'll expose myself if and when my partner is deeply honest and open." This can block inner honesty for an entire lifetime! It's the other person's problem whether s/he is honest or not. You hold yourself back in creating your own experience of love and oneness if you choose to cop out on inner honesty. And this includes complete honesty with yourself.

Always remember that you're learning to communicate deeper and deeper levels of inner honesty to improve your own experience of life. You're doing this to release yourself from a self-imposed jail. You're doing this to open up your own heart. The purpose of inner honesty is not to manipulate or "teach" your partner—although your ego will often try to use your openness and frankness to pressure your partner to change. You're opening up only for yourself—not as a way of helping your partner. But when you are open and honest about your feelings, your partner will find it easier to be open.

Sometimes you hide your innermost feelings because you don't want to work on what you will get in touch with when your partner reacts. Another ploy that the ego uses to keep you from creating inner honesty in your relationship is your addictive fear of hurting the other person if you are totally open. In the past, when you were honest, you may have bought into your partner's stuff. You took responsibility for the anger s/he triggered when your openness activated his or her addictions.

As you begin to see this from a higher perspective, you will realize that nothing hurts the relationship as much as the shades of separateness and isolation that keep the love from being really turned on. **The love that total inner honesty can develop is worth whatever pain may be triggered when your honesty**

hits your partner's embarrassment, jealousy, resent-ment, fear or anger buttons—or your own. Remem-ber that it is always your partner's addictions that are the immediate, practical cause of his or her separating emotions—not the things you do or say. If you blame yourself for these feelings, you are buying into his or her stuff. (Be sure to check with the glossary in Appendix I if a key word like "stuff" is bothering you.)

Give your partner the opportunity to take respon-sibility for his or her experience—and to grow from it. When you hide your real feelings from your partner, you're depriving your partner of the realities of life that s/he needs in order to deal with his or her addictions. You're keeping the relationship greyed-out in varying shades of phoniness, unrealness and shallowness. And it doesn't work anyway. Your partner can intuitively sense that something is wrong because we continuously communicate on non-verbal levels.

The more conscious person breaks through the separate-self barrier of non-communicativeness and makes it O.K. to be creating exactly what one is experiencing inside. When we overcome our hesitancy and learn to express our feelings and thoughts, we break through ego's game. This gives our mind a chance to quit triggering these separating feelings. And in the long run this is a very kind thing to do—kind both to ourselves and to others.

As a method for opening up, you may wish to repeat to yourself many times a day: "I open myself genuinely to all people by being willing to fully communicate my deepest feelings, since hiding in any degree keeps me stuck in my illusion of separateness from other people." This is one of the Twelve Pathways that appear in Chapter 12.

As you become more experienced in operating your consciousness in a way that works toward love and oneness, you will find it easier to communicate your deepest feelings. You will no longer let your ego get away with saying, "These are my private feelings." Of course, they're your private feelings—and the private separateness, private alienation, private loneliness and private unhappiness are also your private possessions. The unified-self does not need this privacy.

The feelings you wish to hide are not a part of the unified-self. They are simply programs you are playing out in your head. Imagine that you had a fine stereo set and you put a scratchy record on it. This stereo will reproduce the scratchy record perfectly—and it will sound terrible. Your emotion-backed addictive demands and the separating emotions triggered by the addiction are simply programs that you are playing out. Just as a scratchy record is not the stereo set, neither are you the separating emotions that are triggered by addictive programs in your head—and played out by your body and mind.

Thus, as you grow in consciousness, you'll be able to watch your mind run off all these programs—but you will no longer identify with them. You will simply see them as the runoff of impressions, mental sets or addictive programs that were put into your mind in times past. You don't need to addictively reject the "scratchy records"—but you don't have to play them out for the rest of your life, either. You can begin to let them go in favor of more beautiful programs that play the harmonies of love and oneness of the unified-self.

You can take responsibility for your separating feelings. You can learn to communicate them openly—and gradually learn to not identify with them. Thus you will find it unnecessary to blame either yourself or the other person for the anger or fear that you create within yourself. It's all programs in your head. And you are not your mental programs.

When you communicate your deepest feelings, you don't have to put on a dramatic Hollywood act. Just share openly and non-aggressively, if possible. Use statements that start out, "I am creating the experience of . . . " instead of blaming forms like, "You make me feel . . . . "

Always remember that you create your experience of life. The world does what it does—but your programming in your head creates your experience of "desirable" or "undesirable." Your changeable pattern of addictions and preferences constantly creates your experience of the world. Hiding your deeper feelings keeps you trapped in a world of separateness—and loneliness. By breaking through your hesitation, you can learn to communicate deeper and deeper levels of inner honesty. And this is one of the fastest ways to open your life and your heart to your partner.

We use the term "sharing" to emphasize the

aspect of just opening up and letting someone inside you. It is preferably not blaming, accusing, demanding, rationally proving oneself right and the other person wrong, although these can take place when sharing. **Sharing is just not hiding anything.**

One of the benefits of sharing (whether one-sided or mutual) is **to help your partner** develop a deeper level of trust. Sharing also helps you find the "us" space behind your differences. When the rocky times come in your relationship and both of you are hitting each other on the head with your addictive demands, your relationship may suffer unless there is a deep level of trust that has been built up by at least one of you. By communicating deeper and deeper levels of both inner and outer honesty, you are building a bond of the heart and mind that will help both of you through the tough times together.

10

Ask for What You Want, but Don't Be Addicted to Getting It.

Your ego often creates the illusion that if your beloved were really tuned-in to you and loved you as you think s/he should, s/he would always know exactly what you're feeling and what you want. But do you always know exactly what's in your partner's head? It's probably best to assume that neither you nor your partner is a mind reader.

We usually create problems when asking for what we want. We may not think it's O.K. to want what we want, and our ego may create a separating "me-vs.-you" experience. There are two errors we may make when asking people to give us something, or to do something for us. We may power trip them and come on like a ten-ton truck with a heavy right-wrong, fair-unfair, good-bad approach designed to coerce them into feeling bad if they don't give us what we want. Or we may just retreat into our shell and drop subtle hints of our martyrdom—or we may just clam up.

Neither aggression nor retreat is the answer to a conscious give-and-take that lets us play the game of life with a fun-filled adventurous spirit. As a way of breaking through the separate-self, let's learn **to simply ask for what we want.** Then we begin to notice that it's our own addictions that create the awkwardness we experience.

Often when you ask your partner for what you want, you make yourself feel anxious or fearful if you expect the request is going to trigger your partner's anger or resentment buttons. This is called "buying into your partner's stuff." When you do this, you are emotionally identifying with his or her addictive models of how s/he, someone else, something or you should be. When you buy into your partner's stuff, you enable both of your egos to keep you trapped in an unconscious, separating game. It takes two people to keep this mirror game going.

When you stop buying into your partner's addictions, you can be serene while your partner runs off his or her addictive storms. If you can feel with loving compassion the "problem" of your partner without getting caught up emotionally in his or her predicament, your partner will be spared trying to cope simultaneously with both his or her addiction and yours.

Your emotional tension is always caused by your own addictions—often interacting with another's addictions. Life works best when you work on yourself to handle your addictive demands so that you can be unattached to whether you get what you want or not. A good motto is:

> Ask for what you want,
> Enjoy what you get,
> Work on any difference.

And, of course, "Work on any difference" refers to inner work on your own emotion-backed demands— not to beating on the people around you.

Ever since Freud studied the pernicious effects of repression and suppression, we have been aware of the importance of giving our feelings an outlet. If we don't do something with the emotion-backed energy that our body produces in response to the stress of anger or frustration, it's like sweeping the dirt under a rug. Repression makes things phony, it keeps us from loving ourselves and others, and can lead to ulcers, high blood pressure and other psychosomatic problems.

We've thus learned to begin **expressing** our feelings instead of **repressing** them. It's a lot better for our mental and physical health to ventilate our anger or act it out in one way or another. But this is not the most skillful use of our emotional energy. Although it temporarily vents the steam, we still have the addictive emotion-backed demand that makes us vulnerable whenever people are not meeting our addictive programming. We're like a time bomb waiting to explode whenever someone pushes our buttons. People who "unconsciously" express their anger, fear and frustration can be vulnerable to the illusion that the world is doing it to them—and thus their lives are characterized by confusion, throwing people out of their hearts and a yo-yoing between pleasure and pain.

What is the way out? **We create problems both by suppressing our feelings or by "blamingly" expressing them. The human alternative is to use this emotional energy to uplevel addictions to preferences.** With preferences, the problem of repression or expression doesn't come up. We've removed the cause (addictions) and not just dealt with the effects (anger, fear, etc.). To sum up, repressing our feelings **is the bottom of the barrel; expressing our feelings hostily, aggressively, and without taking responsibility for creating them is better than repression—but it still creates many problems. But when we uplevel addictions to preferences, we don't continue to create separating feelings to either repress or express. Only this inner consciousness growth offers us the finest possible fruition of a human life style.**

Now is a good time to point out that until you uplevel your addictions to preferences, **your consciousness growth requires that you learn to express your feelings.** And you have to keep expressing your deeper spaces with your partner **so**

you can use this experience for growth. You can't play it phony and pretend you don't have addictions when you really do. This slows your growth.

Instead you work on yourself to progress from a blaming, right-wrong, aggressive expression of addictive feelings to a **sharing** of addictive feelings. When you share, you consciously express your feelings with a non-rejecting "look at what is happening in me." Sharing is an invitation to both you and your partner to look at your inner worlds together—preferably with acceptance and compassion and with insight into the inner work yet to be done. Sharing can set the stage for eventually upleveling an addiction to a preference.

So when the guideline says to ask for what you want, "but don't be addicted to getting it," **we are not talking of repressing your addictive demand.** Not being addicted usually means that you've been working on your head to reprogram your patterns of desire. Then when you ask for what you want, you are simply sharing preferential space.

Often we ask for what we want in a way that implies blame or right-wrong if our partner does not give us what we ask for. Or we may feel, "I've been real courageous and up-front by asking for what I want, and you'd better reward me." We can see this as manipulative and unskillful, for it is a product of the separate-self that reflects a "me-vs.-you" consciousness.

A more skillful and unifying way is to ask for what you want in a way that gives people an opportunity to enjoy giving you what you want—but with a vibe that shows you are not addicted to getting it. In other words, you might ask yourself,

"Am I trying to make my partner feel bad if s/he says 'no'?"

"Am I offering my partner a chance to feel good by giving me this gift?"

"Am I putting out preferential vibes so that my partner will not feel pressured?"

Thus you can be generous in giving your partner a chance to give to you. But keep your addictions out of the way. Addictions keep the scene heavy-handed, neurotic and "deep down" when it can be light, open and lots of fun.

11

Develop Your Awareness of the Constant Beauty and Perfection of Yourself and Your Partner.

One of our biggest impediments to creating an enjoyable life is that we've filled our heads with a number of addictive models of how we should be to experience ourselves as beautiful, capable and lovable. Our egos keep pushing addictive models on us by continually whispering to us, "Your survival is threatened and you need to be different." We usually don't let ourselves create the experience that we're O.K. the way we are. Our egos thus keep us maintaining an act to impress others with our models of how we think we ought to be.

That's O.K. if we want to continue to create and live in a phony world. Almost everybody else seems to be doing the same thing in one degree or another. But it's a drag to keep worrying about other people seeing through our mask. As long as we're preoccupied with this stage image of ourselves, we can't have the fun of enjoying ourselves as we play our roles in the melodrama of our lives—with an accepting, relaxed attitude toward all of the things we like about ourselves and the things we don't like about ourselves.

This is often clear when we look at another person. We can see the self-image that s/he is addictively protecting. We can see how s/he is demanding never to make a mistake, to have a nose that doesn't bulge out, to always remember things correctly, to dress in a way that people approve of, etc. But when we love people, our eyes penetrate beyond the surface and we see deeper than their "act."

As our hearts open, we have the ability to see the preciousness of the beautiful beings that are always behind the mask of personality that they choose to wear. If we're not stuck with our addictions, **we know that our partner is lovable even with his or her addictions.** We sense that s/he would be much happier if s/he would just accept himself or herself, and make it O.K. to occasionally forget things, have a bulgy nose, or whatever.

Our egos are usually busy creating the illusion that we would be beautiful and life would be perfect if about a dozen things could be corrected—about oneself and one's partner. This illusion focuses our sharp rational minds on everything but the real problem—which is always the heavy stock of addictive demands that are programmed in our heads.

One of the most loving things you can do for your partner is to help him or her experience himself or herself as a beautiful, capable and lovable person when s/he opens up freely. There will be times when you can genuinely say, "Yes, I know you don't like what you did and are rejecting yourself. But it's all O.K. Be gentle with yourself." At first your partner won't really believe you because the security addictions that make a person self-reject are very powerfully defended by ego. After a while, your partner may become aware that your acceptance is genuine—and s/he really is O.K. Your partner may gradually begin to discover in himself or herself the beautiful being that is behind the facade of body, mind and personality. In other words, the drama of life can go up and down—but s/he doesn't have to go up and down. You can help your partner develop a self-image that behind the drama, we are, in our essence, always beautiful, capable and lovable.

Thus when you deeply love other people, you clearly experience how O.K. they are as human beings. Your own addictions may not yet let you see that the same thing applies to you. But you too are beautiful the way you are, with all of your foibles, failings and flatulence. And who knows—if you can successfully help your partner accept himself or herself when being genuine, perhaps your partner will someday be able to help you to accept yourself as beautiful, capable and lovable when you are being genuine.

Our addictive demands make us unable to love ourselves and others unconditionally. Our egos thus keep us from experiencing the beauty and perfection of the daily stream of happenings in our life. Using its addictive filters, the ego-mind creates the experience of beauty and perfection only when the here-and-now conforms to the pattern of our addictive demands. We forget that the gratification of these demands is not the only form of the beauty and perfection that life offers us—it is only one form.

Perhaps the deeper and more important form of the beauty and perfection of life is **the opportunity for consciousness growth that we set up in our lives.** For example, we create the experience of satisfaction when the fondue turns out perfectly—and tastes superb. But this gratification is only temporary, and we are still left with our vulnerability to making ourselves upset when the fondue flops. And you know how life is—we win some and we lose some.

As we grow in consciousness, we develop an awareness of the constant beauty and perfection of life when it offers us an opportunity to work on our addictive models. In terms of our long-term happiness, it is more important to get rid of the vulnerability created by our addictive models than to gratify them another time. The former gives lasting enjoyment—the latter only temporary pleasure.

Everything is a gift of the universe—even joy, anger, fear, jealousy, frustration or separateness. **Everything is perfect either for our growth or our enjoyment.** Our ego usually hides this perfection from us during our first stages of consciousness growth. When we're mad at someone, we usually can't see the perfection of it all. We create the experience that they're doing it to us. When we realize it's our own addictions that are doing it to us, we begin to experience our relationship more consciously. That which we experienced as a source of pain in our relationship can really become a source of gain. Our relationship will constantly act as a mirror. We have the illusion of seeing the other person, but what we are really seeing reflected back is both our own beauty and our own hang-ups. Our relationship will be a constant reminder of where we are stuck with an addiction and are flowing energy through the separate-self.

So part of the beauty and perfection of our relationship is that it helps us realize that the other person is not the cause of our irritation, fear, jealousy or anger. **The other person only helps us get in touch with our own internal models of how it all must be for us to let ourselves enjoy our life.** Since life is the way it is, getting the most love and happiness from life depends on the speed with which we can constantly dissolve our emotion-backed models of how it all should be—so that in the now moment, **we can emotionally accept what is.**

In this split second of **now** we can do nothing to

change "what is." So let's relax our emotional muscles. **Let's enjoy what's now.** And from this space we can put energy into consciously making any change we want.

As our skill grows, we begin to appreciate our partner as essential to our own growth. Our partner need not even be aware of this—or try to help us with our growth. In fact, attempts to play "teacher" when one is not being asked to do so may retard our growth. It is part of the perfection of life that in the normal living out of our desire systems, **we will automatically keep on the griddle that part of us which is most raw and most indigestible—and needs cooking.**

As you more sensitively attune yourself to the demands that are keeping you from creating a continuously happy and loving life, you will more deeply appreciate that the person you have chosen as a life partner is particularly adept at helping you get in touch with your addictions. (I'm sure you've noticed!) Your ego had hoped that the relationship would be perfect for your enjoyment—but enjoyment must be preceded by handling your vulnerabilities to irritation, anger, fear, jealousy, resentment and boredom. Once you've handled your addictive demands, you will increasingly experience the constant beauty and perfection of both yourself and your partner—for your enjoyment of the journey through life. But life is like making a cake. First, you've got to put the ingredients together and bake it. Then you get to enjoy it.

12

Surrender to Doing Your Inner Work Within the Relationship by Upleveling Addictions to Preferences.

Some of us have such big addictions that they rival the Himalayan peaks, and some of us have smaller mountains to conquer. These addictive programs continually act like sand in the gears of life. When we become skillful at recognizing addictions and not putting our energy behind them, we can enjoy our remaining years in a state of higher consciousness characterized by more energy, increased perceptiveness and a lot more love—with happiness and joy thrown in as icing on the cake of life.

In Chapter 6, we briefly mentioned that our minds can get caught up in an addictive snarl which is a set of strong, multiple addictions. These snarled addictions are interrelated and support each other. An addictive snarl has roots in the unconscious mind, where we harbor self-rejecting "core beliefs" or unexamined programs, such as, "I am unattractive, incapable and unlovable." These hidden assumptions were usually programmed into our biocomputers during the first several years of our lives by well-meant (but unskillful) addictive words and actions of the people around us. These unexamined core beliefs or hidden assumptions act like a cesspool of infection in the unconscious mind. They are the source of neurosis. They give a hidden support to many of our addictions that we could otherwise drop more readily in adult life. They are like the 90 percent of the iceberg that lies dangerously concealed under the surface of the sea.

Let's explore the analogy of an iceberg in which the visible 10 percent above the surface represents the addictive material we are aware of. The part of the iceberg below the surface represents addictions and core beliefs hidden in the unconscious mind.

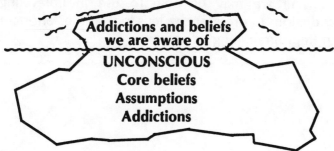

Addictions and beliefs
we are aware of

UNCONSCIOUS
Core beliefs
Assumptions
Addictions

When we do the inner work of letting go of certain addictions, we are working to constantly slice off the 10 percent of the iceberg that is visible and available to our conscious mind. Since addictions create so much pain and separateness (and keep us from loving ourselves and others), our inner work requires that we keep sawing off the 10 percent of the iceberg that is visible. When we get the top part removed, another 10 percent pops up, so that this previously submerged part is now available to work on.

By continually working to uplevel addictions to preferences, we are, in this analogy, gradually removing 10 percent slices of the iceberg as they become visible. This inner work brings an enormous reward. As we uplevel addictions to preferences, our mind becomes a helpful servant to us instead of a tyrannical master that keeps us trapped in a world of illusion and distortion, and butting our heads against the brick wall of reality.

In addition to gradually slicing off the 10 percent of the iceberg that is exposed, it is sometimes possible to blow apart the hidden part of the iceberg which harbors these distorting core beliefs that keep our lives from working well. To understand this possible shortcut we may be able to use in upleveling addictions to preferences, let's look at the "Shortcut in Reprogramming" diagram:

A SHORTCUT IN REPROGRAMMING

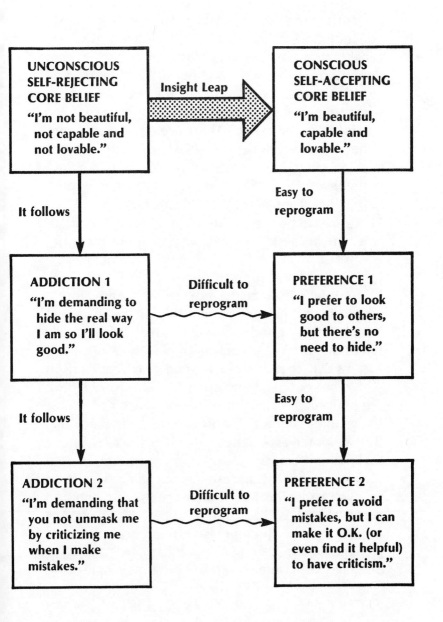

Notice the box labeled "Unconscious Self-rejecting Core Belief" that says "I'm not beautiful, not capable and not lovable." Note the addictions that flow from this hidden assumption: "I'm demanding to hide the real way I am so I'll look good," and "I'm demanding that you not unmask me by criticizing me when I make mistakes." These are not the only core beliefs that keep us trapped in our addictions. The list is often extensive: "I'm not intelligent," "No one really loves me," "Everybody seems to know more than I do," "I am inferior," "I always make mistakes," "I deserve to be fired from my job," "I can't hold on to a mate because I'm unworthy," "My body is ugly," "I can't do anything right," "I should let other people run my life," and so forth—on into the night.

Now let's look at the box entitled Addiction 1, which states, "I'm demanding to hide the real way I am so I'll look good." Our minds may **intellectually** tell us that there is no reason to hide the way we are, that it's O.K. to make mistakes and that in comparison with other people, there are many ways in which we are both superior and inferior—and that it's O.K. for things to be that way for no one can "win them all." But we don't **experience** ourselves this way in our feelings and emotions.

To work on this confusion in our feelings, we must uplevel Addiction 1 to Preference 1, which says, "I prefer to look good to others, but there's no need to hide." But the hidden assumption that we programmed many years ago into the unconscious part of our mind keeps interfering. Our progress in upleveling

72

Addiction 1 to Preference 1 is slower than we had hoped. Notice the wavy line that represents the difficulty in upleveling Addiction 1 to Preference 1. The hidden core belief that we are not beautiful, not capable and not lovable acts as a constant impediment that slows down the inner work of upleveling some of our addictions to preferences. By pinpointing our hidden assumption and exposing it to the light of day, we may be able to work on ourselves to replace "I'm not beautiful, not capable and not lovable" with the nourishing, conscious core belief "I'm beautiful, capable and lovable."

One way to work on yourself to accomplish this "Insight Leap" is to repeat this reprogramming phrase five hundred times per day: "I am beautiful, capable and lovable." This constant repetition may gradually affect the core belief buried in your unconscious mind, and thus undermine the crystallization that holds this self-rejecting assumption together. Instead of shaving off the top 10 percent of the iceberg repeatedly so as to eventually destroy it, in some situations you may be able to blow the iceberg apart by reprogramming the core belief that is causing the trouble. Once you get rid of this undercutting core belief, it will be much easier to uplevel Addiction 1 to Preference 1, and Addiction 2 to Preference 2, etc.

These core beliefs or unconscious assumptions act like pockets of illness in one's brain and constantly make us create false-to-fact perceptions. Let's suppose you are walking down the street and are preoccupied with your own thoughts and thus do not notice me. If I have the self-rejecting core belief "I'm not beautiful, not capable and not lovable," then my mind will automatically compute out an illusion such as, "You don't like me, you purposely shunned me and you don't want to have anything to do with me." But let's suppose I have repeated "I'm beautiful, capable and lovable" 500 times per day for the last three months. Now instead of working from the unconscious self-rejecting programming, I have a conscious core belief "I'm beautiful, capable and lovable." (In our diagram, this reprogramming of a core belief is represented by the bold "Insight Leap" arrow.)

Let's suppose I have reworked my core beliefs in this area so that I can now examine other explanations. Usually people do not ignore someone who is "beautiful, capable and lovable." So my rational mind will now search for other explanations: perhaps you were preoccupied, perhaps you didn't notice me, or perhaps you were in a hurry. Instead of self-rejecting, I realize that "I am not the target." Instead of processing this incident through the "separate-self," which creates alienation, separation and paranoia, I will now process it through the unified-self, which sees things from a mountaintop perspective. I will thus develop a balanced picture of "what is." A unified-self perception can lead me to realize that there have been similar times when I've been preoccupied and perhaps have done the same thing to other people in my life. It's all "us" and I can "love it all" when I get rid of the tunnel vision created by the separate-self, and instead enjoy the panoramic vision of the unified-self.

There may have been many times in your life when you have done things that gave you "proof" that you are not beautiful, not capable and not lovable. Your self-rejecting tapes may have been triggered when you forgot an appointment, burned dinner or got in a scrape with the car. **But these things are not proof that your self-rejecting core beliefs are right.** You are always beautiful, capable and lovable in your essence as a human being. Forgetting an appointment or anything else is just a happening that does not alter your continuous beauty, capability and lovableness. You may do things that are not beautiful, not capable and not lovable—**but in your essence you are always beautiful, capable and lovable.**

Thus, your unconscious self-rejecting core beliefs and addictive programmings are like clouds hanging over you in all of your activities. A beautiful part of a living-with relationship is that it helps you uncover these destructive mental programmings so that you can work on them more effectively. To take advantage of these opportunities for growth, it is helpful to work on yourself every day in a systematic way. Here is a daily practice that can make an enormous difference in your life:

1. **READ THE HANDBOOK:**
   Each day slowly and meditatively read five pages in the *HANDBOOK TO HIGHER CONSCIOUSNESS.* Start again when you finish it. Read it over

and over to hear the deeper levels; it is packed with information and techniques for creating a conscious, loving life. The *Handbook* can help you apply the twenty-one guidelines on relationships. You will also find it helpful to reread this book on relationships several times to help you get behind the resistance of your ego in applying it in your life. Appendix III contains "Our Way to Happiness," which is a helpful review of the Living Love Way.

USE THE TWELVE PATHWAYS:
Memorize the Twelve Pathways and say them before arising and after going to bed. The Pathways are a neat capsule containing the life principles that can show you how to open your heart and tune in to your intuitive wisdom. They are an important part of the essence of Living Love. It is extremely helpful to say them slowly to yourself whenever you are upset.

SHARE YOUR INNER FEELINGS:
Before going to bed each night, take a few minutes to develop insight into your addictions by sharing with your partner. It is important to acknowledge your addictions during this sharing. Be aware of your tendency to work on the other person's head or tell him or her how wrong s/he is. Pinpoint specific emotions and addictions you experienced during the day. Which of the Twelve Pathways applies to today's addictions? Are you sharing the things your ego wants to hide? That is

THE TWELVE PATHWAYS
To Unconditional Love and Happiness

FREEING MYSELF

1. I am freeing myself from security, sensation, and power addictions that make me try to forcefully control situations in my life, and thus destroy my serenity and keep me from loving myself and others.

2. I am discovering how my consciousness-dominating addictions create my illusory version of the changing world of people and situations around me.

3. I welcome the opportunity (even if painful) that my minute-to-minute experience offers me to become aware of the addictions I must reprogram to be liberated from my robot-like emotional patterns.

BEING HERE NOW

4. I always remember that I have everything I need to enjoy my here and now—unless I am letting my consciousness be dominated by demands and expectations based on the dead past or the imagined future.

5. I take full responsibility here and now for everything I experience, for it is my own programming that creates my actions and also influences the reactions of people around me.

6. I accept myself completely here and now and consciously experience everything I feel, think, say, and do (including my emotion-backed addictions) as a necessary part of my growth into higher consciousness.

INTERACTING WITH OTHERS

7. I open myself genuinely to all people by being willing to fully communicate my deepest feelings, since hiding in any degree keeps me stuck in my illusion of separateness from other people.

8. I feel with loving compassion the problems of others without getting caught up emotionally in their predicaments that are offering them messages they need for their growth.

9. I act freely when I am tuned in, centered, and loving, but if possible I avoid acting when I am emotionally upset and depriving myself of the wisdom that flows from love and expanded consciousness.

DISCOVERING MY CONSCIOUS-AWARENESS

10. I am continually calming the restless scanning of my rational mind in order to perceive the finer energies that enable me to unitively merge with everything around me.

11. I am constantly aware of which of The Seven Centers of Consciousness I am using, and I feel my energy, perceptiveness, love and inner peace growing as I open all of the Centers of Consciousness.

12. I am perceiving everyone, including myself, as an awakening being who is here to claim his or her birthright to the higher consciousness planes of unconditional love and oneness.

important. If your partner is not available (or does not want to participate), write what you are telling yourself in a journal.

If you are consistently doing this three-part daily practice and feel that you are not breaking through an addictive snarl fast enough, it may be helpful to attend a Living Love training. These intensive trainings (offered on a non-profit basis) will give you practice in applying the Living Love Way in your everyday life. (See Appendix II for information on where trainings are available.)

Be kind to yourself and don't use the long-term project of upleveling addictions to preferences (and the short-term project of more consciously handling addictions when they come up) to create another way to criticize or reject yourself. See it as a challenging consciousness game (played by your separate-self and your unified-self). This game has the greatest of rewards—the creation of more love and happiness in your life.

13

Be Open to the Form the Relationship Offers.

There is no form to the spirit of love. Each society offers its inhabitants a set of social forms. These social forms (known as mores, conventions or "the right way to do things") may or may not fit the life situation and desire systems in which partners find themselves. Since it's a game we're playing with ourselves, and these social forms often change within a generation, one may not wish to addictively live out every social form offered by one's society. On the other hand, a conscious person will not be caught up in being a rebel for the sake of rebellion, either. It is usually O.K. to do what we want to do—provided we do it non-aggressively and don't force our way on other people. It helps if we consciously experience our actions as a part of the growing unity and oneness of everything.

One of the social forms that often pushed my relationships into a cliff-hanging mode had to do with whether we would be monogamous or have sexual relationships with other people. My partner tended to want the former while I usually opted for the latter. This came up in every long-term relationship or marriage that I had. I finally had the wisdom to hunt for the way out.

I began to notice that the pleasure I got in the occasional sexual experiences outside of the relationship was not as great as I expected it to be. And it took so much energy and planning to bring these outside intimate relationships into fruition—usually with so little fruit.

I also began to notice that most couples who were open to outside sexual activities did not stay together very long. Monogamy is not a guarantee of permanency —but it can be a great help. It simplifies the addictive demands that are triggered between two people. I gradually became aware that time after time (even when we agreed on sexual freedom at the beginning), the jealousy my partners experienced kept them from creating deeper levels of trust and involvement with me. It didn't pay off in creating the great adventure of life together.

I finally decided to let go of my unworkable models and instead be **open to the form my relationship offered. I began to let my partner decide whether the relationship was to be sexually open or monogamous.**

This enabled me to tune-in to the full beauty and

perfection of what I did have in my relationship. When I let go of controlling the form of the relationship, I began to get more of what I really wanted—a flowing experience of cooperation, love and creating the great adventure of life together. Thus by becoming open to the form that my relationship offered, I learned to bypass a swampy area in my life in which I was often pulled into the quicksand.

By dropping my addictive demands for sexual variety, and focusing more energy into making the most of the mutual sexual energies, I now find I can create far more unity with my partner and much less separateness—and more fun too!

How do you determine the forms of your relationship? You want one thing and your partner wants another. The answer to this will boggle your rational mind—but the deeper intuitive part of you will sooner or later be able to hear it: **You surrender; but you do not give a "gift" you cannot afford to give.** And when you try to live out both of these simultaneously, you will be face-to-face with the inner work that your life is offering to you to get free.

No one knows all of the answers to how we should manage our day-to-day activities—either individually or as a group. We are processes—and the world is a process. Actually there are no single final solutions. We should therefore be open to carefully considering or trying out the form a relationship offers.

On the spiritual plane, however, the guidelines are very clear: our own thoughts and actions which feed our inner experience of selfishness, separateness and addictive demands will trap us and keep us from loving ourselves and others; our own steps toward acceptance, cooperativeness, trust and generosity will help us work toward love and oneness. And it's only through continually creating the experience of love and oneness for ourselves that we can get the most that's gettable from our lives.

14

Discover the "Us" Place in Terms of Surrender, Compassionate Power and Mutual Give-and-Take.

Our egos have somehow created the illusion that we shouldn't let other people tell us what to do—that it's better to play "Chief" (the commanding role) than to play "Indian" (the supporting role). All of this is in the realm of illusion because "Chief" and "Indian" are only parts that we play in the drama of life—they are not who we really are. Who we really are is a precious essence of humanity; we all have a human heart that beats and feels; we all have a conscious-awareness, which is an essence of the being that watches the drama of life go by. And at this level of looking at human life, there are no "Chiefs" and there are no "Indians"—there is just us, and we are all alike in our essence.

Our egos in their constant tendency to amass more security, more sensation and more power, pride and prestige, keep us addictively trapped in identifying with who we aren't—rather than who we are. Any good actor knows that it is not as important to play a particular part in a drama as it is to select a part that reasonably fits his or her talents—and then play that part as skillfully as possible. It's much better to play a supporting role like Iago than to bumblingly act out the leading role of Othello. Often it is wise to play well the part that is now available—and to practice patience until a new role is available or our skill has developed or we have learned to want the role we have.

When life is seen from a perspective that is undistorted by ego, we realize that it really doesn't matter whether we play the part of Indian or the part of Chief. From the panoramic view, we can clearly see that **we are not any of these roles. We are a precious essence beyond and behind all parts in the drama.** So we can tell our egos to stay out of it. In each situation in life, we can try to find the part that best fits us—and that will coordinate with the overall harmony of the melodrama of our lives.

We therefore need to look carefully at the three modes in which human beings can organize themselves to get the world's work done. We can then consciously choose whatever role best fits our talents and that harmonizes with the other actors and actresses. We remind our egos that the greatest satisfaction comes from perfectly playing our role—

rather than trying to grab a certain type of role and identify with it. So let's look at these three modes of relating to other people in the games of life:

1. The Chief Role. When you elect to play Chief, the game is to play a wise Chief. This means that you will use compassionate power when needed with the Indians that you are leading. It's power from the love center used to benefit everyone—not power to enhance your separate-self. Although you stay open and listen to suggestions from the Indians, it's up to you as Chief to decide. If an Indian wants to take over your role as Chief, you just regard that as life's way of checking out your ability to lovingly play the Chief role. Firmly, but with loving, compassionate understanding, you decide what's to be done, and you see that the Indians carry it out. Constantly arguing about who is Chief, or bickering over the best way to do something, is confusing and can lead to everyone losing. The Chief is not fulfilling his or her leadership function if s/he timidly lets things fall apart. If you're cast in the Chief role, play the role fully and without hesitation—but don't get ego-identified with the role. It's not who you are.

2. The Indian Role. The role of the perfect Indian is to surrender to the Chief. As pointed out above, this does not mean that a good Chief will not welcome facts and suggestions from the Indians. In the perfect Indian role, we flow supportive, creative energy and suggestions to the Chief without being addicted to the Chief acting on them. The group benefits most when Indians play Indian, and give the Chief the energy and support needed to carry out Chief-type

decisions. Since Oscars are also awarded to actors who excellently play supporting roles, the game is to tune-in your ego to playing the Indian (or supporting) role perfectly. In a way that is not addicted to one's own aggrandizement, the Indian role requires that one be conscious of the job the Chief is doing with an awareness of when a new Chief is needed by the group.

3. The Indian-Indian Game, or Flowing With Peers. In many life situations it is not appropriate for either partner to be cast in the Chief or the Indian role. Then we can use the Indian-Indian relationship. A skillful playing of this role involves learning to flow with another person. To play this role, you tune-in your mind to compromising and cooperating to discover the course of action that gives each of you the most that is jointly gettable—all things considered.

When egos stay out of the way, it's usually obvious how we can flow as Chief, Indian or Peer in a spirit of harmony and love. The thing to remember is that none of us is really a Chief and none of us is really an Indian. These are just roles that we are playing in the drama of life. The game is to play out these roles consciously and flexibly and to find a satisfaction in playing well whatever roles we are cast in.

In a marriage relationship, you will probably play all of these roles simultaneously. For example, you might play the Chief role when it comes to gardening, and your partner could play the Indian role and help carry out decisions that you've made about where to put the fertilizer. Because of his or her skills, your partner might be well cast in the Chief role in preparing meals and your job would be to play perfect Indian in the kitchen. In the area of making decisions about the children, both you and your partner might elect to play the Indian-Indian game. This would mean that neither of you would play a Chief role or an Indian role. Instead you keep looking at each situation to find the way that cooperatively offers the most harmonious, give-and-take balance in each situation.

A safe way to play the Chief-Indian-Peer game is, in each situation, to play Indian-Indian until your partner agrees (verbally or otherwise) to play Chief or have you play Chief while s/he plays Indian. Remember, fewer addictions are triggered by playing Indian-Indian than by assuming the "Chief" role without an agreement.

Of course, these roles are not to be set in concrete and carried out mechanically over a period of a lifetime. When one disengages one's ego from insisting on playing Chief all the time, it can be fun to play either Chief or Indian. And it may add to our conscious enjoyment of our soap operas to pass these roles around so as to get as much variety and experience as possible.

Life gets much simpler when we do not get caught up in security, sensation, power, pride and prestige addictions. **We open the doors of happiness when we let ourselves consciously enjoy playing the roles our life gives us in each moment.**

We have now completed the seven guidelines for

creating a delightful relationship. Skill in putting these together is essential—and comes only with insight and practice. Since some relationships may go beyond the point of no return, the next section presents seven guidelines for altering your involvement **but without sacrificing love.** I hope you won't need these additional guidelines—but here they are if you do.

Part Three

Seven Guidelines
for Altering
Your Involvement

15

Alter Your Involvement If You Do Not Want to Cooperate Together in The Great Adventure of Life.

In the first chapter of this book, it was suggested that you approach your relationship as an opportunity to cooperate in the great adventure of life. If you or your partner do not want to continue cooperating, you will not be able to experience your life together as a great adventure. In its place will be a dreary, dutiful drag.

Of course, your core beliefs and emotion-backed demands will always be at the root of your troubles together. Changing an addiction to a preference acts like magic in clearing away clouds of separateness and dissension. **But always be gentle with yourself. You're a human being, and it's normal to have programmed**

addictions. A very important part of your inner work is to emotionally accept yourself just as you are—addictions and all. You have to be realistic and face the fact that sometimes you can change addictions to preferences—and sometimes you won't be able to handle it. If month after month, you or your partner are unable to handle the separating stuff that is being created by your core beliefs and addictive programming, and if you have lost your energy for cooperating in the great adventure of life together, your mind may lead you to consider changing your involvement.

Let's use the term "changing your involvement" instead of talking about ending the relationship. Actually there is no way to end your relationship with the person you've been living with. As fellow voyagers on planet Earth, you are in a relationship with everyone else on the earth. You breathe the same air, drink from the water supply of the planet and are inextricably related socially, economically, politically, culturally and otherwise. So, when seen from a broad point of view, relationships cannot be terminated—they can only be altered in the quantity and quality of your involvement.

In Chapter 8, we described the four states of relationships that are generated by your patterns of involvement and addictions. If you no longer wish to cooperate together in the adventure of life, you may decide to switch your state of relationship to one with less involvement and less addiction. This may enable you to develop a warm lifetime friendship together.

16

For Your Own Growth, Consider Staying in the Game Until You Have Upleveled Your Addictions to Preferences.

When you stand back and look at your life from a panoramic perspective, you can see that it is your addictive demands that keep you from enjoying your relationship. Your ego and mind want to blame your partner. But the fact is that changing partners may not be all that helpful. For you're still stuck with your particular pattern of addictive demands, expectations and models of how things should be. The chances are that when you settle in with a new person, in one way or another, you'll be running the same tapes that can be predicted to create the same problems in the relationship. So, sooner or later, you might as well battle your addictions.

Suppose you are engaged in a battle in which you have two allies and one enemy. Including yourself, that's 3-to-1 odds. Pretty good situation. **However, let's suppose that you do not recognize your allies, and instead mistake them for enemies.** And then to make matters even worse, let's suppose you don't recognize the true enemy at all. Since you don't recognize your enemy, it is hidden by your ignorance. So the enemy operates in the open— continually slashing at you and hurting you. Your response is constantly to mistake the source of the pain, and to lash back at your allies instead of the real enemy. So because of your tactical mistakes, you are creating odds of 3 to 1 against you. Your chances in such a battle are awful.

And that's our predicament. Our allies in our consciousness growth are the people outside of us— and ourselves. But we often mistake them as enemies and blame "the enemy outside" or "the enemy inside" for our anger, fear, irritation, jealousy, resentment and unhappiness. We blame other people for "doing it" to us—not realizing that in the normal course of their lives, they are only providing us with the painful "teachings" we need to work on our addictions. Or if we are self-rejectors, we blame ourselves—not realizing that we are our own best friend when we know who we really are.

The greatest tragedy of this confused fog in which we try to live our lives is that we don't recognize the real enemy. For the real enemy is not the people and situations outside of us—nor is it ourselves. The real enemy is our addictive emotion-backed demands, which are the immediate, practical cause of all of our separateness, alienation and unhappiness. Unless we carefully learn to recognize our addictive programming as the intervening variable between the outside world and our experience, it will continue to do its dirty work of cutting us up, and making us think that something else is doing it to us.

If your living together hasn't yielded happiness, take responsibility (without blaming yourself) for your experience, and dedicate it to your apprenticeship in learning the lessons of life. Don't lose out on the opportunity for consciousness growth that a stormy relationship offers you. Consider staying in the relationship to work on upleveling your addictions to preferences—or at least learn to see them consciously.

Use this opportunity to share with your partner on the deepest level you can. Share your gut-level stuff—and don't be addicted to your partner hearing it without triggering some of his or her addictions. Keep working on your head.

But if your addictions seem too rock-like, and you just can't get on top of them, make it O.K. to decide not to continue playing the game of living together. The situations in our daily lives offer us the fire that enables us to burn out our addictions. But this doesn't mean that you have to work so close to the fire that you burn yourself. The game is to cook your addictions—not you.

17

Take Responsibility for Altering the Relationship—But Don't Blame Yourself or the Other Person.

Remember that you played your part in setting up the relationship, you lived in it and you are now playing your part in altering the involvement. Try to understand that the other person is not doing it to you. You are each creating your own experience of what is happening. Each of you plays an interrelated role of acting and reacting to your own and each other's addictions.

It will help if you don't buy into the ideas produced by your rational mind, which will always do a good job of making you right and the other person wrong, making you fair and the other person unfair, making you consistent and the other person inconsistent. Our minds are great at encouraging our egos to feel good with all this rationalizing, but that's not where the wisdom lies. Remember that your relationship has been a joint interaction between two people. Try not to get caught up in the illusions of guilt, self-rejection, blame, jealousy, fear, anger, resentment and other separating states of mind.

You don't have to conduct a trial in your head—in which you play the part of prosecuting attorney, judge and jury. It's not necessary to convict your partner of heinous crimes in order to make it O.K. for you to alter the form of your involvement. You want to be able to look back on what's happened and appreciate the beautiful things that you've shared together. Look at the donut—and not the hole.

There's no need to convict your partner and then sentence him or her to banishment from your life. You don't have to play the scene this heavy. You entered into the relationship—it was your choice. You can alter your involvement in the relationship if you don't want to cooperate together any longer in the great adventure of life. You can keep it simple, compassionate and loving.

Altering the form of your relationship can be done with love and mutual cooperativeness—or you can act out soap opera scenes of blaming, vindictiveness and vengeance. I'd like to share a beautiful letter I received from David W. McClure, who is a minister of the Unity Church of Truth. In this letter he communicated that he and his wife, Barby, were separating. Here is the letter:

Dear Friends:

One of my favorite phrases from Kahlil Gibran's book, *The Prophet,* is one that I use often in weddings I perform:

"But let there be spaces in your togetherness,
And let the winds of the heavens dance between you.
Love one another, but make not a bond of love:
Let it rather be a moving sea between the shores of
your souls."*

Last month I shared with you the news that my wife, Barby, had decided to release herself from involvement in the church and seek her own career and identity elsewhere.

I must now share with you that we have reached a time in our marriage relationship where it has become necessary for us to "let there be spaces in our togetherness." After a great amount of time and prayer, we have decided in an atmosphere of love and mutual respect, to divorce.

As I write this letter I am reminded of something Eric Butterworth wrote: "Certainly in our vast experience in counseling, we (as ministers) have discovered that marriage partners do not always grow at the same rate or even in the same direction. One of the great confusions

---

*Reprinted from *The Prophet* by Kahlil Gibran with permission of the publisher Alfred A. Knopf, ©1923 by Kahlil Gibran; renewal ©1951 by Administrators, C.T.A. of Kahlil Gibran Estate and Mary G. Gibran.

of our society is the assumption that two people will always and forever be able to force their lives into one mold."

Barby plans to remain in Spokane for the time being and pursue her new career. I trust that all of you who have been and are her friends and supporters will continue to give her your love and active friendship even through these changes in our personal lives.

I intend to continue as your minister and to give myself enthusiastically and wholeheartedly to serving you through this ministry.

Each of you is very special to Barby and me, and we want to thank you for the positive, loving thoughts and supportive prayers you have given us during this time of transition.

Lovingly in Unity,

David

So take responsibility for altering your involvement. You're running an addiction if you're blaming yourself or another person. Blame is an attempt of the separate-self to keep you energizing the addictions that play a part in causing the change in your involvement. Through your unified-self, you can welcome this opportunity to learn the lessons of life so that you will not have to repeat them.

18

Be Totally Open and Don't Lie or Hide Things.

Trust is needed in reducing the involvement in a relationship just as much as when you are deciding to live together or are living together. The problem with lying or hiding things is that these activities **make you feel increasingly separate** from your partner or ex-partner.

And then you'll have to live with this illusion of separateness you've created. It can dominate your mind and color all of your thinking. In extreme cases, your addictions can make you reinterpret all the beautiful things that happened in the relationship and create a sourness in their place. Take responsibility for your experience. No matter what's happening, **you always create your experience of happiness or unhappiness, beauty or ugliness, heaven or hell.**

If you can, resolve to create a situation where both of you win. Focus on both of your beneficial intentions rather than your addictive demands. Don't tighten into a "me-**vs.**-partner" confrontation. Instead, do your inner work to hold on to a "me-**and**-partner" way of looking at the soap opera of life as it goes by. There is always a human, caring way to sort out whatever comes up in the drama of decreasing your involvement together.

This may mean lots of communication to be open with how you feel—and especially what you are afraid of. Don't let your pride get in the way. Use the form "I feel (*specify your emotion*) because (*state what's happening*) which can have the effect of (*say what you don't want in the future*)." This simple form can help your partner understand your feelings of fear, resentment, anger, frustration, terror, insecurity, and separateness. Try it!

Above all, don't blame yourself for anything that happens. Decreasing your involvement does not mean anything about you. It's all a matter of your programming clashing against your partner's programming. There are life lessons in this for both of you.

All of the details that need to be handled when two people decide not to live together any longer can become very complicated and unpleasant if mutual trust and cooperativeness has been destroyed. Contrary to the usual way it's done when separation or divorce is happening, life is giving you an opportunity for openness and generosity. Treat your ex-partner as you would treat a brother or sister that you love—and the rest of your life will be richer because of your understanding and generosity.

19

Follow Through on Your Commitments or Work Out a Change in the Commitments.

In your journey toward higher consciousness, you start from where you are right now. And if where you are right now involves such commitments as children or debts, you treat these as something established in your life and you work with them. It can be deeply separating when another person relies on your commitment and you ignore it. This adds to the cynicism, alienation and distrust in our world. And we have enough of that already. If you've made a commitment, your inner work on yourself involves carrying through on this commitment unless you can renegotiate it one way or another.

Perhaps your life is trying to give you a message about making commitments too rapidly or too wildly. Commitments always involve a claim on your future energy and time. You know that the world changes and your melodrama changes. On the other hand, some of the more worthwhile games of life require you to make certain commitments. So you have to learn to find your path between too much and too little.

Whether you are going into a relationship or becoming less involved in a relationship, it's important to cautiously examine the commitments you make to another person. It won't work if you try to lasso a person into a relationship by promising things you know s/he wants to hear. Give what you can give—but don't give what you can't wisely afford. All too often we're willing to verbally or non-verbally commit ourselves to much more than we are willing to do when the chips are down. This always comes as a shock to our partner for s/he was most likely counting on us to follow through on our commitments. This will lower the trust and make us feel more separated and alienated from each other.

You don't have to meet all the addictive or preferential models of your partner. In fact, you can't. And your partner can't meet all of your desires, either. It's O.K. to be real—and to recognize your limits. Don't let your partner depend on a phony you. Don't let your partner coerce you into doing, saying or promising something you cannot live with. But once you have committed yourself, try to follow through or work out a change in your agreements. A mad rush of addictive rights, wrongs, shoulds, shouldn'ts, fair, unfairs, goods and bads follows when you or your partner ignore commitments. Often you create the illusion that your life is just barely balanced and will work as long as "everything" is in place. When you can compassionately understand your partner's predicament (it could be your predicament), you can more cooperatively and tenderly renegotiate whenever you feel it is necessary. And it will sometimes be necessary!

So follow through on commitments that you have made as a way of honoring and loving yourself or work out a change in your agreements. Remember that you do this to create a more livable world for yourself—and more livable inner feelings. For you have to live with yourself and appreciate yourself—no court will give you a divorce from yourself.

20

Work to Stay in the Love Space, for Only This Will Enable You to Make Wise Decisions.

When you are decreasing your degree of involvement in a relationship, you'll probably have a wonderful opportunity to work on yourself to stay in a love space. You may have the chance to demonstrate your skill in operating your mind by creating the experience of love for someone who is angry with you. Or perhaps you will get to test your skill with someone who tries to hit your addictions which make you trigger feelings of hurt, or who lies about you to your friends. All these happenings in the melodrama of decreasing involvement enable you to check out your ability to love everyone unconditionally—including yourself.

If you addictively maintain that the only way to change your involvement is to "fight your way out," you set yourself up for unnecessary separateness and suffering. I remember reading about a divorce attorney who advised his client against the high cost of what he wanted to do. The client replied, "I don't care what it costs or even if it takes all my money. I just want to hurt her." When you create this experience, you not only deprive yourself of money, but also of the understanding, cooperativeness and helpfulness that an ex-partner may be able to offer you in the friend role for the rest of your life. Don't shortchange yourself.

When you or your partner, or both of you, choose to decrease your involvement, a lot of addictive stuff will come up. Some of your strongest security, sensation and power addictions that have only been lurking around your mind will jump out like tigers and tear at you. And how about all the supporting actors and actresses in the melodrama of your lives—relatives, parents, friends, children, and the neighbors next door? Each will have his or her set of "right-wrong" programmings that s/he will gladly offer you for free. If you don't keep your head and heart in the love space with your partner, you will buy into such stuff and get trapped in vengeance, hatred, guilt, distrust, "getting even" and other separating illusions.

You can take responsibility for your part in creating the relationship; you can take resonsibility for your part of what came up in the relationship; and you can take responsibility for the part you are playing in altering the form of the relationship.

Please note that taking responsibility is something that is very different from blaming yourself or others. Don't get caught in the blaming trap. It's only when you keep your heart in the love space that you can use your internal wisdom (that is always there) to come through the separation experience or divorce proceedings in a way that makes you feel taller—and more capable of dealing with the rocky territory that we all encounter in life's journey.

Hold on to your heart space—even as you put someone out of your home! For when you throw someone out of your heart, your mind will then see him or her through distorted addictive filters. If you hate someone, you won't recognize even the considerate things s/he may say or do. The wellsprings of your perception will be poisoned by your paranoia. Your prophecy of "s/he is rotten through and through" becomes self-fulfilling when you build an addictive wall between you and another person by your negative actions, distrust and hatred. A clear perception of "what is" that is undistorted by anger or fear is wiser and more genuinely protective to you than any addictive melodrama.

21

It's Only a Melodrama—So Don't Get Caught Up in It.

When you decided to enter into a relationship with your lover, you probably found lots of social approval. Most people smile and say, "That's nice," when you tell them of your plans to play house together. But except for a few close friends, most people feel they're supposed to express regret and sympathy when you are changing your involvement. So it's up to you to stay conscious, and not feed your friends' tendencies toward blame, judgmentalness and resentment—and the illusion that a catastrophe is happening.

Remember it's all soap opera. If it starts to feel serious, check over your addictive demands. Relationship is only a life game that we play together. If you've worked on yourself to make it a preference to be deeply involved rather than an addiction, you'll be able to play this scene in your life consciously and lovingly.

What if you want to end your relationship and your partner is still addicted to the relationship? If this happens, just lovingly work with the situation—back and forth. You may have the opportunity to work on your impatience. Listen carefully to what your partner is saying to you and repeat it back non-judgmentally so that s/he feels that you have heard. Lovingly and clearly continue to express how you see the evolving situation. Be open to looking at your own addictions that make you want out.

People who blame other people or themselves for their experience in life are caught in a trap that bites tighter and tighter. Here are the phases that will pinpoint your steps in getting free of the blaming trap:

1. The Blaming Phase. The books you read, shows you see, the conversations with other people and your early home and school upbringing usually taught you to blame other people for your experience. It's even codified in our language forms: "You make me angry when you do that." "The boss scared me when he asked how I liked my job."

Blaming other people for your internal experience creates the illusion that your happiness is dependent on the thoughts, feelings and actions of other people. Every passing wave of life crashes over you and leaves you floundering. This is nonsense. It's always your programming in the form of your addictive demands that makes you trigger the experience of unhappiness. And you needn't blame yourself. Just use everything for your growth. (At this point it could be helpful to reread chapter 5 to get a deeper level of insight regarding the vital importance that your programming plays in creating your experience in life.)

It's possible for you to go to the next step in creating a more enjoyable life when you have the insight that it's always your addictive or preferential programming that creates your feelings and thoughts—your happiness or unhappiness. This insight gives you the energy to let go of your addictive demands—and make them preferences.

2. Taking Responsibility Phase. Once you realize that your addictive demands are the immediate, practical cause of your illusion of separateness, you will begin to take responsibility for your experience (and let me caution you again, taking responsibility does not mean blaming yourself). When you've had a direct experience in a life situation that your addictive programming (which is inside your head) is basically your only problem and that working on it is basically your only way out, you can begin to pick up speed in your journey of growth. You'll find simple solutions that were always within you—but were blocked from your awareness by your addictive programming. Life will begin to go into a new dimension, and you will more deeply live in the awareness that love is more important than anything else in life. You will see your life as a melodrama—as not serious—and at the same time you will realize that each moment you set up consequences that you will be dealing with in the next step in your life.

3. Creative Cause Phase. In this phase you realize you choose what you get in life. You realize that you're not a victim, you're not just responsible for your experience, but you actually co-create your soap opera. What does it mean to be a creative cause of your life? Here's an example from my life. In my second marriage, I had an addictive demand that my partner not be depressed one or more days every week. When my mind ran off its blaming habits, I would say, "Bonita makes me unhappy when she is depressed." I placed upon her the responsibility for my enjoyment of life and I was certain that I was right—she was doing it to me! I was stuck in the blaming phase and it tore our marriage apart.

Now here's how I escaped from the blaming phase: As I became more aware of how my consciousness worked and how my ego-mind created a stream of illusions based on "self-**vs.**-her" programs, it was possible for me to increasingly have the insight, "When she is depressed, I think it means something about me. Now I know that it is my addictive demands that make me reject what she says and does at these times. I thus can take responsibility for the resentment and frustration I feel because it is my own programming that is creating my experience."

This opened the doorway for me to advance to the third phase in which I saw myself as a creative cause of my life experience. I could tell myself, "I chose to go into this relationship with Bonita. I get to work on my addictive programming that makes me vulnerable when she says or does certain things. I see that I co-created the relationship by choosing to enter into it, and I now realize that I can get free of the feelings of separateness by working on my own head. I now see that I am the creative cause of all my experiences. Likewise Bonita is the creative cause of all of her own experiences. We both create this for our growth —so I'll benefit by it and take the growth."

This third phase of experiencing yourself as a creative cause helps you avoid being caught up in resisting, fighting, blaming, criticizing, and creating all sorts of separating experiences. It enables you to tune-in to your inner power to be a godlike creator in your journey of birth, life and death.

Part Four

Loving Unconditionally

22

What Is Love?

What is love? How do we recognize the experience that the word "love" points to? In a way it's somewhat like explaining the sensation of the color "purple" to a blind person. If we have not experienced purple, words are of little help. If we have experienced purple, words may not be necessary. Thus, if we had never experienced love, it would be of little use to read a chapter full of words on love. These words would not be able to point to something in our experience that would be helpful.

Fortunately, we are not in the situation of a blind person who has never experienced the color of purple. Some of us may keep ourselves on a starvation diet with this important vitamin of the soul, but at some time or another, we've experienced love. So let's continue our exploration of what the word "love" points toward.

Another thing that complicates answering the question "What is love?" is that we mix love with many other types of human experience. This can confuse us when it comes to sorting out exactly what we mean by "love." For example, we can have sex without love, or we can have sex with love. Since our society often frowns on sex without love, one may tend to mix up the experience of sex and the experience of love. Such an experience can be beautiful, and there's nothing wrong with mixing them together in our minds. But this blending of sexual energy and love may make it a little more difficult for us to sort out exactly what the word "love" points to in our human experience. Similarly, our feelings of love may be colored by feelings of respect, envy, jealousy, insecurity, power dominance, dependency or pride. Just as water may offer us many different experiences depending on whether it is mixed with tea, gin, coffee, lemon and sugar, or chocolate and powdered milk, so love may be experienced in many blended contexts. It is nevertheless possible to acquire a clear idea of what water is like when it is pure. It is similarly helpful to explore what the word "love" points to when it is not mixed with other human experiences.

In the Living Love Way, we do not experience love as a feeling that we "should have" for ourselves and other people. Instead we find that love springs spontaneously into our hearts and minds when we work on our emotion-backed addictive demands that a person be different from the way he or she is here and now. In other words, we work on the subtle (and not so subtle) psychological desires and requirements that can control the doors of our perceptions. We see our addictive demands as filters that muddy one's perception of oneself and others.

Emotional acceptance is a key to creating the experience of love. This means the willingness to be with things as they are for the rest of our life. But remember that emotional acceptance also does not exclude one's working with "what is" in order to change it. It just means that the motivation for changing it does not consist of desperately trying to get rid of a situation that triggers our emotions of anger, disgust, fear, jealousy, resentment, irritation or boredom. Instead of creating an urgent survival experience around our addictive desire to see something changed, we enjoy the many benefits of preferential programming. It's like "Let's see what the game of life feels like if we play it this way instead of the way we've been playing it." And since we've learned to accept the life fact that **we win some and lose some,** we can play the meta-game of trying to change our games without being addicted to whether the game changes or not.

So we see that one of the keys to the game of loving is to become aware of the ways in which we are demanding that people be different from the way they are. And instead of putting addictive energy into trying to change them (which usually brings about resistance from the other person), we learn that it is far more effective to put our determination and energy into just letting go of our addictive demands. When we uplevel an addiction into a preference, we see afresh the words and actions of another person—uncolored by our addictive demands. This break-through can create a totally new experience. In the words of the Third Patriarch of Zen, "For when a thing can no longer offend, it ceases to exist in the old way."

Meher Baba, a conscious being who died in 1969, told us, "Love cannot be born of mere determination, for through the exercise of will one can at best be dutiful. One may through struggle and effort succeed in bringing his external actions into conformity with his conception of what is right, but such action is spiritually barren, without the inward beauty of love. Love has to spring spontaneously from within; it is in no way amenable to any form of inner or outer force. Love and coercion can never go together; but though love cannot be forced on anyone, it can be awakened through love itself. Love is essentially self-communicative: those who do not have it catch it from those who have it. Those who receive love from others cannot be its recipients without giving a response which, in itself, is of the nature of love. True love is unconquerable and irresistible and goes on gathering power and spreading itself, until eventually it transforms everyone whom it touches. Humanity will attain to a new mode of being through the free and unhampered interplay of pure love from heart to heart."*

*Reprinted by permission from *God to Man and Man to God* by Meher Baba. ©1975 by Adi K. Irani.

Many years ago I remember hearing Ram Dass mention "loving everyone unconditionally." At that time I had only a limited understanding of love. It was largely based on our cultural norms. I found this concept of "loving everyone unconditionally" quite strange. It seemed to me as though it would not be love if applied to everyone. Love was something special that could only be experienced with one or a few people in one's life at the same time. Can I love a business associate the same way I love a person I'm married to? As I began to work on my addictive demands that made me create the feeling of separateness in my life, my heart began to open. Over a period of several years, I gradually began to experience that it is possible to love everyone equally—but not to be involved with everyone equally. Thus, the quantity of the love experience will be many times greater with the person I live with—**but the quality of the love experience can be the same with everyone.**

One of the first breakthroughs in understanding how one can love everyone equally came as I mentally separated sexual desire from the experience of love. Since my sexual orientation is toward women, my mind had been operating in the usual form in our culture that a man could not feel love for other men. When I saw that I could love without sexual involvement, I opened up the possibility that I could create the experience of love for other men. Thus, by disassociating sexual energy from love energy, I found that I could really feel love for other men. And when I looked at this experience of love, it seemed to me that it was exactly the same experience of love that I felt with a woman to whom my heart had opened. And it felt really good to have at last broken through a barrier that kept me from experiencing love with half of the people on this earth!

But I was still stuck in a high degree of selectivity. Just as I could create the experience of love with only a few women, I was still creating the experience of love with only a few men. As I continued to work on upleveling my addictions to preferences, I began to see how the addictive programmings in my head played a large part in determining whom I would let myself love, and with whom I would block the feeling of love. Then it became clear that all I had to do was to sweep away these addictive programmings of my mind to become more and more open to love. I began to see how it is possible to "love everyone unconditionally—including yourself" even though I was a long way from doing it consistently. It's just a matter of inner work and has nothing to do with what other people say and do.

And that was my next step in opening my heart to love—to make sure that the door of my heart did not slam shut when someone said or did something in the melodrama of life that did not fit my addictive programming. In working on myself in this area, I found it helpful to see the acts of myself and other people (and the entire melodrama that we are creating together) as just a run-off of the tapes in our heads. Our words and actions are not who or what we really are. Behind all of the melodrama—**here we**

are — a precious essence of humanity—and divinity. We are a consciousness-awareness that is watching the entire show from the top of the cosmic mountain.

I began to see that it's O.K. for me to play my part in the melodrama of life by throwing someone out of my territory—**but there was never any need to throw anyone out of my heart.** On the stage of a theater, the actors may consciously fight each other—like playing a game. But it would be unfortunate if these actors were angry offstage just because the onstage script called for a fight in Act 2. You play your role, but it would be sick to identify with it.

As I began to create an experience of my life as that of an actor in a cosmic game in which I was both a playwright and an actor who played many parts, I could then see other people with greater perspective—and wisdom. I could increasingly tune-in to the beautiful being **that's really there inside them** behind all of the melodrama of their lives. This helps me to avoid addictively responding to the thoughts and actions that people are mechanically playing out.

Most people unconsciously identify with their set of mental habits called "personality" and "social roles." But in spite of how they look at themselves, I found that it is always possible to look beyond the surface appearances to make contact in my heart with the beautiful being inside them that is always there.

The most socially helpful action you can take is to work on yourself to love everyone unconditionally— and especially yourself. **The tuned-in social cooperativeness that flows when we love everyone as a**

brother or sister is the only way to solve the immense planetary problems that we have created by living out our addictive, separate-self tapes. Only a wise integration of the reasoning of our heads and the love in our hearts will save us. We've got the head—now let's work on our hearts to deeply get in touch with our love space.

Love is not only a shortcut to harmony and happiness in living together—it is the only route. Love creates an energy of selfless service. Love enables us to feel good in giving our time, thoughts and possessions to another person. As our love becomes purer (freed from selfishness or gain for ourselves), we begin to feel such a unity with other people that we do not create the experience of our separate-self giving something to "them." It's all here in the world. It feels as though we are just a conduit to sort things out to put them where they are needed. As we create less of an experience of "me" as a separate self, and tune in more to the reality of "us" as a part of the unity of the whole world, we experience that our life has its amplification and expansion in loving and serving others.

We discover that whenever our ego expects something in return, we lose the essence of love. For love cannot be like a business deal based upon barter or equal exchange. Our own life can demonstrate that when we give selflessly and openly to other people, we begin to create a loving field around us in which we get back much, much more than we could ever give. But this magic of love will not happen if we take a bookkeeping attitude.

The unconditional love of oneself and of all others enables us to create an experience that is absolutely priceless and cannot be fully attained through any other means. Only by using love as the means, as well as the goal, can we fully transform the pettiness and unsatisfactory quality of our experience of life.

Over and over again we receive letters that say in one way or another, "The books I read tell me how great my life would be if I stayed centered and loving all the time. But I didn't know how to do it. The *Handbook to Higher Consciousness* told me how to do it."

And once we understand about love, and resolve that it is more important than anything else, the next step is to begin the inner work on ourselves. **The desire to love is, by itself, only the first step.** The ability to love everyone unconditionally (and especially oneself) must be developed **by practicing it with consistency and determination using the situations in our lives.**

There are many approaches to consciousness growth—and there is a common thread running through each. However we choose to do it, the most enjoyable human lives are characterized by energy, perceptiveness, humor, insight, wisdom, happiness, purpose and love. **These dependable satisfactions are created BY DECREASING OUR ADDICTIONS AND INCREASING OUR LOVE. Only this inner work opens us to the full joy of living.**

Appendix I
Glossary

ADDICTION: An emotion-backed demand, expectation or model that makes you upset or unhappy if it is not satisfied. It may be a demand on yourself, on another person or on a situation.

ADDICTIVE DEMAND: Another term for addiction.

ADDICTIVE SNARL: Multiple and/or conflicting emotion-backed demands. Snarls are usually kept going by beliefs or unconscious assumptions that are generally hidden from your awareness.

ADDICTIVE TAPE: The words and phrases you have programmed that automatically run through your mind when you are feeling separating emotions.

BUYING INTO STUFF: When you emotionally identify with (or emotionally reject) another person's addictive models of how s/he, someone, something or you should be, and create separating feelings in yourself.

CAUGHT UP: Uptight. Feeling any separating emotions. Running addictive tapes.

CHANGING THE "OUTSIDE WORLD": Putting energy into changing situations or people (including yourself) that you wish to be different, as contrasted with doing the inner work of upleveling your addiction to a preference.

CLEAR: Having no addictive demands triggered; feeling completely accepting; not creating any separating emotions.

COP OUT: To consciously or unconsciously avoid acknowledging, looking at or working on a demand. To deal with an easier or safer issue rather than handling what is really bothering you or what is difficult for you to face.

COP TO: To share "stuff" you would normally hide; to admit; to be open and honest about.

EGO: The master controller of your mind that

determines what is processed onto the screen of your consciousness. The ego is your friend, but it often operates from separating, addictive tapes and false-to-fact core beliefs. These create the illusory experience of the separate-self whose domain of security, sensation and power is continually threatened by "what is." As you retire these separating tapes by working on your addictive programming, the ego activates tapes that let you experience the unified-self that transforms your experience of yourself and of the world around you.

EGO-MIND: A compound term referring to the joint operation of the ego (when it selects which addictions are being threatened) and the rational mind (when it searches for solutions to protect the addictions by creating "me-vs.-them," "right-wrong" and "subject-object" thought forms). The ego-mind thereby continually maintains the illusion of the separate-self.

FEEDING AN ADDICTIVE DEMAND: Satisfying your emotion-backed addictive demand instead of using the Methods to uplevel it to a preference.

GAME: An activity of life that has do's and don'ts and a win-loss position. "Game" refers to the roles we play in life, e. g., the marriage game, the parent game, the consciousness growth game, the insurance game, the sex game, etc. This meaning of "game" should not be confused with the way in which it was used in *Games People Play* by Eric Berne, which refers to dishonest ploys that we use to manipulate another person. When we play life as a game, we can avoid the heaviness of a "right-wrong" judgmental approach and instead create an effective and enjoyable experience of life.

INNER WORK: The process of consciously using the Living Love Methods to gain insight, uplevel your addictions to preferences, and love unconditionally.

LOVE: Emotional acceptance is both the goal of love and the means toward the goal. The experience of love is created when our perception is not being distorted by "me-vs.-them" perceptions. Love is the experience of others as "us," and not separately as him, her or them. Addictions are the enemy of love. Love increases when we handle our feelings of criticalness and separateness from ourselves and others.

MELODRAMA: Your "act"; your actions on the stage of life. The purpose of this term is to help you experience the moment-to-moment events in your life as though it were a play or drama production. This helps us see our here-and-now in perspective and with detachment instead of creating threatening self-conscious addictive perceptions that keep pushing our emotional buttons.

MODEL: An expectation. A particular form or standard of how you, someone else or a situation "should be" or "shouldn't be." Models can be either preferential or addictive.

PAYOFF: Some psychological, emotional or physical reward that can induce you to hold on to an addiction. Payoffs may be real or imaginary.

PREFERENCE: A desire which is not backed up with any separating emotions or tensions in the body or mind. It is a preference if you do not create any separating emotions or thoughts when you do not get what you want. From a preferential space, you can put energy into making changes, but you are not attached to the results and remain unconditionally accepting and loving of yourself and others. Preferences help us experience life through the 4th, 5th and/or 6th Centers of Consciousness.

RATIONAL MIND: The function of your brain that analyzes, justifies and reasons. It is activated by ego to protect security, sensation and power territories. The rational mind becomes our master when it is perpetuating a consciousness of the separate-self. It is our servant when it produces perceptions from the point of view of the unified-self.

"REAL YOU": Your conscious-awareness; your essence as a human being as distinguished from the changing processes of your body, mind, emotions, thoughts, social roles or actions.

RIPOFF: The ways in which holding on to a demand keeps you from feeling loving, being effective and enjoying your life. Your suffering and unhappiness. Getting less than is available; negatively affecting, e.g., "rip-off energy."

SEPARATE-SELF: The illusory "me-vs.-them" perceptions that guard your security, sensation and power addictions. The mental programs that create the experience of one's life as a battle against oneself, other people and the world instead of the compassionate, understanding, and wise flowing of energy through the unified-self that sees how it all fits into a common pattern of individual and social growth and enjoyment.

SEPARATING EMOTIONS: Feelings such as fear, disappointment, anger, hurt, boredom, loneliness, guilt, unhappiness, etc. that create the illusion of alienation from yourself and/or other people.

S/HE: To be read as "she or he."

STUFF: Separating emotions such as fear, frustration and anger. The chains of rationalizing, criticizing, judging, and blaming thoughts and actions that are triggered by one's addictions. Also see "buying into stuff."

TAPE: Your verbal, emotional and bodily responses to life situations. Words that go through your mind; programming in your biocomputer. Tapes may be preferential or addictive.

TEACHER: People, situations or objects that put us in touch with our addictive programming. Consciousness growth requires that we open ourselves to the "teachings" that occur in the daily interactions of life.

TUNE-IN TO: Become aware of; listen to; explore or experience.

UNIFIED-SELF: "Us" instead of "me-vs.-them" programming. Programming that gives us an overall perspective of how everything fits perfectly into our journey through life, either for our growth or our enjoyment. The unified-self thus creates an experience of people and situations as a unified or integral part of our journey instead of a nuisance or threat.

"WHAT IS": What you are choosing to addictively reject (which may be a real or imagined situation). "What is" also refers to impartial, objective reality; the way the universe is unfolding as contrasted with the illusory versions you create by your addictive demands.

Appendix II
Workshops for
Personal Growth

The Ken Keyes College in Coos Bay, Oregon offers a variety of personal growth workshops. Depending on your needs and interests, some are as short as a weekend, many are five-day courses, and some are longer. All of the trainings are designed to show you how to break through your personal roadblocks to enjoy your life more fully. The emphasis is on the practical application of the "Science of Happiness" in your daily life—instead of knowledge alone.

The Living Love Way emphasizes increasing energy, awareness, love, and the joy of living. The lives of over 20,000 students, housewives, businessmen, teachers, counselors, doctors and others have been enriched by the workshops we have developed. The courses include room, board and instruction at nonprofit prices which run about one-half the usual cost of other workshops.

People are discovering that the "Science of Happiness" is effective—regardless of the "up-and-down" circumstances presented by the world in which we live. Once you have learned to make the Methods work in your life, you will be able to devote yourself to a deeper level of inner work which will heighten your enjoyment of life and improve your interactions with others. The workshops cover such topics as relationships, marriage, sexuality, conscious parenting, career, communication skills, money, relating in business, body and health, and spirituality. Besides helping you define who you are, you will be learning to accept and appreciate yourself more. Many people come for one training and stay for several. All of the life-expanding trainings give you an opportunity to discover more about yourself and allow you to grow in ways that help your life work better.

You'll love your visit to the beautiful city of Coos Bay located on scenic U.S. 101 on the Oregon coast. It has the third largest harbor on the west coast of the United States with many attractive beaches. Across the street from the College there are public tennis courts and jogging trails. Within a half hour drive there are spectacular waterfalls and the Oregon Dunes National Recreation Area. The College is easily accessible by car, bus or air.

To get a catalog

For a free catalog of workshops and other courses offered by the College, send your name and address to Registrar, Ken Keyes College, 790 Commercial Ave., Coos Bay, OR 97420. Without charge you will receive a quarterly catalog listing nonprofit workshops, books, audiotapes and videotapes. If you wish more information about the trainings, you may phone the Registrar at (503) 267-6412.

Books by Ken Keyes

About two and one-half million copies of Ken Keyes' books are now in print. They are distributed worldwide and several have been translated into many languages. Appendix IV contains a list of his books that are available through local bookstores or from the Ken Keyes College Bookroom, 790 Commercial Avenue, Coos Bay, OR 97420. You can order using Visa or Mastercharge by calling (503) 267-4112.

For workshop schedules, a free catalog of books and cassettes, or to get on our mailing list, write or phone:

Ken Keyes College
790 Commercial Avenue
Coos Bay, OR 97420
(503) 267-6412

Appendix III
Our Way to Happiness

Our way to happiness is open
when emotion-backed demands are mastered.
The automatic triggering
of fear, frustration and anger
makes us robots
instead of creative causes
in the changing energies of life.

The ego and intellect combine,
demanding more, more—and yet more,
and our experience of life is wanting.
We strive and toil and scheme,
and shove and complain and resent.
But pleasure and satisfaction are temporary
and our illusion of separateness seems real.

As we learn how our consciousness works,
we discover the opening key.
Our desires and demands and requirements
act as a distorting screen
filtering what is happening
to warp our experience of now.

The beauty—the ugliness
the safe and the threatening
the good and the bad
the fame and the shame
the loss and the gain
the pleasure and pain
are merely what we're programmed
to reject or accept.
The wide gulf
between these polarities of life
lies not in the world outside
but only in our heads.
Was addictive or preferential programming
used to create our experience
of the here-and-now?

To demand what we don't have,
is to waste what we do have.
To take offense from what's happened
can destroy our happiness.
In the changing world of people and things,
we win some and we lose some—
regardless of knowledge, fame or money.
As we free ourselves of addictions,

the winning and losing
becomes only a game
in which we can
LOVE IT ALL.

Security, sensation and power demands—
these create the deepest illusions.
They waste our insight and energy,
and destroy our ability to love.
When at last we understand
how we do it to ourselves
and create the world we experience,
we can live an awakening life.

As cause and effect,
we link our insistent addictions
with all of our suffering.
When we're clear about this
an enjoyable life is possible.

Demanding and rejecting,
criticizing and judging,
"righting" and "wronging"
are the sicknesses of the mind.
To be free of distorted perceptions,
see the chains of addictive patterns
that dominate our consciousness
and make our lives a battle.
Our perception of others
is only our projection
of fears and desires for ourselves.
By seeing our models as not needed,

the people we meet are not spewed
with our fears, frustrations and angers.
We know them more consciously as "us"—
not separately as "him," "her," or "them."

Two steps are crucial
to live a life of love:
First, see our self-imposed prison,
and then, resolve to be free.

Everyone now is a teacher
and all of our life is a teaching—
this is the fastest route.
Everybody and everything
help us on our way.
When we experience offense,
life offers us our next step
in doing the inner work.
When we create feelings of joy,
life is giving us a taste
of living in a world of love
that ever beckons us onward.

The day-to-day practice
of the method of your choice
opens the way to freedom
and a life of living love.
To continue reading and shopping
only builds ego's defenses
and stops you short in your growth.
Beyond a certain point,
more knowledge is only fettering.

Placing a price tag on love,
or bartering one demand for another,
keeps us shaky, and always vulnerable
to irritation, resentment and anger.
But when love is unconditional
our experience of life is transformed—
and a life of bliss is ours.
For nothing that is said or done,
can make us feel separate again.

And love without strings
applies also to oneself,
for we are always lovable
and the world has a place for us
exactly as we are.
Always accept and love oneself—
without conditions
without judgments
without condemning
without hiding.
We are O.K. the way we are—
even with our attachments.
We won't be "better"
if we reprogram our addictive models.
It's just that we'll enjoy our lives
much more when we do.

To live in this new world
of continuous wisdom and love,
we must change our expectations
and love ourselves and others

*just as we are
or as we are not.*

*We may wish to avoid people's games
but we always know their hearts—
which are just like ours.
Involvement may be conditional;
but love is never withheld.
In the dramas of life,
we may throw someone
out of our territory,
but never out of our heart.*

*Thus love is a bridge
from heart to heart
from being to being
while the games of life play on.
So we learn to flow
in harmony with all around
as we fully attune to the Law—
the Law of Higher Consciousness:
Love Everyone Unconditionally—
Including Yourself.*

*As our heavy load
of demands is lightened,
we increasingly experience
the perfection of life.
In our essence we're always perfect,
though the programs we play out
may yield pain and separation.
The world around us is perfect, too—*

offering us either a perfect teaching
or the perfect opportunity
to enjoy our here-and-now.

See how the intellect
acts as a "yes-man."
It helps us play out
the roles of personality
with which we have learned
to blindly identify ourselves.
These roles are only habits;
they are not who we really are.
For behind the drama of our lives—
father, mother, child,
boss, worker, doctor or cook—
there lies the awareness
of our consciousness.
Behind all our drama—
HERE WE ARE!

If you would transform the world,
start within yourself.
Let the Pathways be your guide—
unfolding beyond the sterility
of unapplied knowledge.
In the give-and-take of life,
saying these Pathways whenever upset
gives us a space
to transcend our hang-ups.
They tune us in
to our inner wisdom
that we continuously smother

by our alarms and our fears.

How simple this is!
Just to say the Pathways
when we make ourselves feel separate.
But notice how the ego—
abetted by the rational mind—
stops us in this easy practice
and keeps us trapped in acting out
the tragedy of our lives.

We get the most from our days
when we change our tortuous demands.
Upleveling addictions to preferences
leaves us invulnerable to suffering
yet open to joy and happiness.
Becoming more deeply confirmed
as we surrender our addictive desires,
we experience the "cornucopia" of life.

We discover at last
what eluded us before:
insight, perceptiveness, wisdom,
joy, fulfillment and happiness,
a calm mind,
tuning in to our higher self,
and the continuous experience
of loving ourselves and others.
We are now invulnerable
to the changing drama,
and we no longer alienate ourselves.

We have suffered enough.

*We no longer choose
to create and inhabit
a world of separateness.
We will free ourselves—
and our brothers and sisters—
not by force, but by example,
by working on ourselves,
and loving and serving the world.* *

*A cassette is available containing "Our Way to Happiness" (shared by Ken), and The Twelve Pathways (shared by Bill Lentz). To order this send $6 plus $1.25 for postage and packaging to Ken Keyes College Bookroom, 790 Commercial Ave., Coos Bay, OR 97420.

142

Appendix IV
Other Books by Ken

Handbook to Higher Consciousness
Ken Keyes, Jr.
Perfectbound, $4.95

Why are our lives filled with turmoil and worry? Why do we allow ourselves only small dribbles of peace, love, and happiness? The *Handbook to Higher Consciousness* presents practical methods that can help you create happiness and unconditional love in your life. These methods can be used in your everyday life to feel peaceful and secure—despite all the conditions surrounding you. Countless people have experienced a dramatic change in their lives from the time they began applying these effective techniques explained in the *Handbook*. Over three-quarter million copies in print.

Gathering Power Through Insight and Love
by Ken Keyes, Jr., Penny Keyes, and Staff
Perfectbound, $6.95

Here's how to do it! This outstanding book gives you detailed instructions on exactly how to develop your loving spirit. It describes the 2-4-4 system for advancing the transition from the separate-self to the unified-self. It is essential for those who want the most rapid rate of personal growth using the Science of Happiness.

How to Enjoy Your Life in Spite of It All
Ken Keyes, Jr.
Perfectbound, $5.50

Each one of the Twelve Pathways has an entire chapter devoted to it. These guidelines offer you detailed insights for creating a more enjoyable life. Step by step, you are shown how to take the Pathways from the printed page and make them dynamic tools for bringing increased energy, perceptiveness, love, and inner peace into your moment-to-moment living.

Taming Your Mind
Ken Keyes, Jr.
Clothbound, $7.95

This enjoyable book (which has been in print for 35 years) shows you how to use your mind more effectively. It can enormously improve your success in making sound decisions. It is written in an entertaining style with about 80 full-page drawings by the famous illustrator Ted Key. It was previously published under the title *How to Develop Your Thinking Ability* and was adopted by two national book clubs. There are over 100,000 copies in print.

Prescriptions for Happiness
Ken Keyes, Jr.
Perfectbound, $3.95

Treat yourself to more happiness by having these three prescriptions handy! They can help you tune-in to your own self-worth—your right to an enriched life—and can help you put more fun and aliveness into your interactions with people. Designed for busy people, this book can be absorbed in a little over an hour. Ideal for gifts.

How to Make Your Life Work or Why Aren't You Happy?
by Ken Keyes, Jr., and Tolly Burkan
Perfectbound, $3.95
In a light and entertaining style, Ken offers this timely message with cartoons on every other page for people who want to improve the way their lives are working. Its easy style makes it simple for a beginner, yet deep enough to offer insight for all. Many folks feel as though it had been written expressly for them.

Your Heart's Desire—A Loving Relationship
Ken Keyes, Jr.
Perfectbound, $3.95
Do you want to bring the magic of enduring love into your relationship? All of us have had a taste of what heart-to-heart love is like. We cherish those times and strive to experience them continuously. Using your rich inner resources, this book can help you to create a more loving relationship—without your partner having to change! It offers support for you to beautifully deepen the harmony, love, and trust you now enjoy.

The Hundredth Monkey
Ken Keyes, Jr.
Pocketbook, $2.00
There is no cure for nuclear war—ONLY PREVENTION! This book points out the unacceptability of nuclear weapons for human survival. It challenges you to take a new look at your priorities. With the intriguing concept about the power of our combined efforts, it shows how you can dispel old myths and create a new vision to save humanity.

Available in bookstores or from Ken Keyes College Bookroom, 790 Commercial Avenue, Coos Bay, OR 97420. Send payment with your order, including the shipping fee of $1.25 for an order up to $9.95. Please add $1.25 for each additional $10 in the order or specify UPS collect for the shipping charges. You may order using VISA or MasterCard by phoning (503) 267-4112.